Known by Our Love

Known by Our Love

Celebrating the Spirit-Filled Life

www.FamilyChristian.com

Published by Family Christian Stores, 5300 Patterson Avenue SE,
Grand Rapids, Michigan 49530.

ISBN 1593910223

1 2 3 4 5 6 7 8 9 10

Dear Valued Guest,

For more than seventy years, Family Christian Stores has had the privilege of impacting lives for Christ as a ministry-minded business. For this reason, we take extra care to offer one of the widest selections of Christian products designed to strengthen the hearts, minds and souls of believers and seekers from all ages and stages of life. This book you now hold in your hand is an extension of our mission. The *Hearts, Minds & Souls* series is an exclusive collection of books created to engage our guests in transforming and redemptive relationships with our Savior, Jesus Christ.

In addition to this book, the over ten thousand different products available in our stores and through FamilyChristian.com website provide a wealth of additional resources to address every need from a faith-filled, Christ-centered perspective. We have Bibles for everyone from young children just learning to read to seminary students serious about every nuance of Greek and Hebrew. We even have Bible accessories like covers, highlighters, tabs and more. We have books for men and women, singles and married couples, kids, tweens, teens and adults. We have music to minister to the hearts of every rhyme and rhythmical preference. From cards to tees, household items to framed art, pens to games, whatever your need, we promise you'll find something to enrich and enhance your lifestyle at Family Christian Stores.

We're also sensitive to your desire to be a good steward of the resources God has given you. That's why we offer a price matching promise, exclusive Perks program and great monthly deals on the latest most popular books and music.

Thank you for shopping Family Christian Stores and FamilyChristian.com. We appreciate your partnership in reaching families and communities with the gospel and grace of Jesus Christ. We ask that you pray for us as we seek to operate our company in a way that best fulfills the mission God has given us.

Answering the call to help strengthen
the hearts, minds & souls of our guests,

Dave Browne
President/CEO
Family Christian Stores

FAITH

HOPE

LOVE

Faith

for the Journey

"For we walk by faith, not by sight."

2 Corinthians 5:7 NKJV

1

You Must Face Your Goliath

The greatest discoveries in my own life have come as a
result of adversaries who sought my demise.

By Tony Miller

Usually our first response to adversity is to run from it. We need to
run toward it instead very invitation to greatness is accompanied by
obstacles and mountains that have to be faced. Adversity is
nothing more than an incubator to process the destiny of men and
women who are going to change the course of history.

Many times the very problems we think are going to destroy us
become the platform for our promotion. We don't like to admit it,
but we need enemies in our lives. The enemies we face make us
aware of areas of need in our lives that we would never have
recognized had we not faced the enemy.

Some of the greatest discoveries in my own life have come as a
result of adversaries who sought my demise. And who knows if we
would have heard of David had there not been a Goliath, or of
Moses had there not been a Pharaoh.

Your friends create comfort, but your adversaries bring creative
movement. It is not until we get tired of being harassed or taunted
that we rise up with decisive action to begin the process of maturity and growth. Creativity, boundaries, strategies all are born when
a "giant" appears in our pathway. Our willingness to respond
releases God's power on our behalf.

I know what it is to fight giants that have come to hinder my
progress and try to force me into boundaries of limitation and isolation. Several years ago my wife, Kathy, and I experienced one of
the most devastating attacks of the enemy against our lives and
ministry.

People we had trusted and loved targeted us with their bitterness
and refusal to progress. While experiencing breakthroughs and

fresh anointing on one hand, we were being taunted and harassed on the other. Our adversary was challenging our destiny.

Today, it is not shocking to me that David, after having been anointed king, was brought to a place of confronting a giant. However, when I have confronted them, I thought I was finished. I even prayed to die! Dying, it seemed to me, would have been better than living.

My confrontation with giants had taken place shortly before we took our family to the mountains for our annual Christmas vacation. While there, I slipped into the bedroom and got back into bed, not wanting to face my family or the future. The whole time I was trying to reason with the Lord, the voice of the enemy was heckling my mind. All I could think about was the challenge of these giants.

I whispered a prayer to God: "Father, I am empty, and I don't know what to do. It seems that my enemies have triumphed over me. Maybe I only thought I was called to this place. Somehow, take away this pain inside me."

As tears began to roll down my cheeks, I heard the Spirit of God speak inside me. It was not with blowing trumpets or a cloud of smoke but just a quiet voice, the kind that infuses your spirit with hope.

The Lord said to me: "The anointing that is in you is stronger than any force trying to bind you. Get up, fresh oil is on the way." At that moment I recognized that I was born to conquer those giants. This mountain was going to prove to be the battlefield of victory for my future.

I got up and talked with my wife, who had stood by me faithfully. We decided: "We cannot run from this Goliath. We must face it head-on."

It's pretty normal to desire to run from trouble in life. When you get up in the morning and the voice of your oppressor speaks loudly in your ear, taunting you, daring you to come out or make advance- ment, it is natural to yearn to crawl back in bed and pull the covers over your head.

That is what happened to Saul and the soldiers who fought with him. Every morning they got up and dressed for battle and went out shouting the war cry (SEE 1 SAM. 17:20-21). When Goliath challenged them, they ran in fear to their tents and hid.

How often have you gone out, dressed for the part and saying the right things, only to retreat at the first sign of opposition? Saul's warriors ran to their tents, but we run to our places of self-protection and safety—places of refuge where we will not be confronted or challenged; comfort zones where we make habitual choices and sound progressive, but end up going nowhere!

Comfort zones are no protection against giants. Neither is running from the giant. If you don't run toward the giant and overcome it, you will find yourself running into a life of make-believe success and significance. Before long you will find that your success and significance are nothing more than tattered, worn-out "tents."

Don't cower in timidity from the mocking voices of your Goliaths— run at them instead. But never run at them with your mouth shut! That is a formula for defeat. Declare His name—Jesus! The mention of His name causes the forces of hell to tremble.

With his simple slingshot and a mouth full of confidence, David ran toward Goliath. With one release of the stone, the giant fell. David ran and cut off Goliath's head for the king. A great victory had been won!

Friends, if you are always weeping over criticism and rejection, continually frustrated because somebody misunderstood you, or upset because some group of friends won't let you in their group anymore, you must make the choice to break free today! Your progress and future potential demand it. Don't allow the voices of a few to rob you of His voice saying, "Well done!"

Bio
Tony Miller is a traveling apostolic minister based in Greenville, South Carolina. He recently released his first book, Journey to Significance (Charisma House), from which this article is adapted.

2

Don't Hold On to Your Hurts

Jesus commands us to forgive, yet most of us treat His words
as suggestions. We must learn to release all offense.

By R.T. Kendall

All of us have been wounded at some time in our lives, many of
us deeply. And it's not something to take lightly. People experience
real pain when they or those they love are hurt by another person.
Yet we know that the Bible commands us to forgive—and that
extending total forgiveness to our offenders is the only way we
will ever find true freedom and release.

Certainly if our offenders would put on sackcloth and ashes as a
show of repentance, it would be much easier to forgive them. But
remember, at the foot of Jesus' cross no one seemed very sorry.
There was no justice at His "trial"—if you could even call it that. A
perverse glee filled the faces of the people who demanded His
death: "'Crucify him!'" they shouted (MARK 15:13, NKJV).

Furthermore, "those who passed by blasphemed Him, wagging
their heads and saying, 'Aha! You who destroy the temple and
build it in three days, save Yourself, and come down from the
cross!'" (vv. 29–30).

What was Jesus' response? "'Father, forgive them, for they do not
know what they do'" (LUKE 23:34).

This must be our response as well.

Jesus could have said, "I forgive you." But such words might have
been misinterpreted and wasted, like casting His pearls before
swine (SEE MATT. 7:6). Instead Jesus asked the Father to forgive them,
a far more grand gesture.

Asking the Father to forgive them showed not only that Jesus
Himself had forgiven them and released them from their guilt but
also that He wanted His Father to refrain from punishing them. It

was not a perfunctory prayer; Jesus meant it. And it was gloriously answered! These offenders were among those who were converted after Peter's address on the day of Pentecost (SEE ACTS 2:14-41).

God has given us a mandate in His Word regarding forgiveness: "Be kind to one another, tenderhearted, forgiving one another, even as God in Christ forgave you" (EPH. 4:32). "Bear with each other and forgive whatever grievances you may have against one another. Forgive as the Lord forgave you" (COL. 3:13, NIV).

It's not a suggestion. We must totally forgive those who hurt us.

Totally forgiving someone doesn't necessarily mean you will want to spend your vacation with him or her, but it does mean that you release the bitterness in your heart about what the person has done. We can take our example from the way God treats us.

How does He forgive? Unequivocally and unconditionally. He never holds our sins, which are many, against us or tells others what we did. In practical terms, total forgiveness encompasses all of the following aspects:

1. Being aware of what someone has done, and still forgiving. Total forgiveness is not being oblivious to what an offender did; it is not covering up, excusing or refusing to acknowledge what happened. Total forgiveness is achieved only when we acknowledge what was done without any denial or covering up—and still refuse to make the offender pay for his crime.

Total forgiveness is painful. It hurts when we kiss revenge goodbye. It hurts to think that the person is getting away with what he did and nobody else will ever find out. But when we are able to fully acknowledge what he did and still desire in our hearts that God bless him in spite of his wrong, we cross over into a supernatural realm. We begin to be a little more like Jesus; we begin to change into the image of Christ.

2. Choosing to keep no records of wrong. The Bible says that love "keeps no record of wrongs" (1 COR. 13:5). Love is a choice. Total forgiveness is a choice. It is not a feeling—at least at first—but an act of the will. It is the choice to tear up the record of wrongs we have been keeping.

We clearly see and acknowledge the evil that was done to us, but we erase it—or destroy the record—before it becomes lodged in our hearts. This way resentment does not have a chance to grow.

We must learn to erase the wrong rather than file it away in our mental computer. When we do this all the time—as a lifestyle—we not only avoid bitterness, but we also eventually experience total forgiveness as a feeling—and it is a good feeling.

3. Refusing to punish. Refusing to punish those who deserve it—giving up the natural desire to see them "get what's coming to them"—is the essence of total forgiveness.

Our human nature cannot bear the thought that someone who hurt us would get away with what he has done. It seems so unfair! We want vengeance. But vindication is God's prerogative alone. In Deuteronomy 32:35 He tells us clearly, "Vengeance is Mine, and recompense" (NKJV).

4. Not telling what they did. There is often a need to talk with someone about how you have been hurt, and this can be therapeutic if it is done with the right heart attitude. But if sharing is necessary, choose the person you tell very carefully, making sure that person is trustworthy and will never repeat your situation to those it does not concern.

Anyone who truly forgives, however, does not gossip about his offender. Talking about how you have been wounded with the purpose of hurting your enemy's reputation or credibility is a form of punishing him. We divulge what that person did so others will think less of him.

When I recall that total forgiveness is forgiving others as I have been forgiven, I remember:

▸▸ I won't be punished for my sins.

▸▸ Nobody will know about my sins, for no sins that are under the blood of Christ will be exposed or held against me.

5. Being merciful. When it comes to being merciful, this is our Lord's command: "Be merciful, just as your Father also is merciful" (LUKE 6:36). In the Greek language, mercy is the opposite of wrath or justice.

One difference between grace and mercy is that grace is getting what we don't deserve (favor), and mercy is not getting what we do deserve (justice). So when we show mercy we are withholding justice from those who have injured us, and that is one aspect of godliness.

There is a fringe benefit for those of us who show mercy: We will also be shown mercy (SEE MATT. 5:7). This shows that total forgiveness is not devoid of self-interest. "The merciful man does good for his own soul" (PROV. 11:17).

6. Showing graciousness. True forgiveness shows grace and mercy at the same time. There is an interesting Greek word, epieikes that means "forbearance" or "tolerance." In Philippians 4:5 this word is translated "gentleness."

It comes down to our English word "graciousness." It implies an exceedingly rare act of grace. It cuts right across a legalistic spirit, which is what comes naturally to most of us. This concept is quite threatening to those of us who think that being inflexible for the truth is the ultimate virtue.

Graciousness is withholding certain facts you know to be true in order to leave your enemy's reputation unscathed. Graciousness is shown by what you don't say, even if what you could say would be true.

Self-righteous people find it almost impossible to be gracious; they claim always to be after "the truth," no matter the cost. Total forgiveness sometimes means overlooking what you perceive to be the truth and not letting on about anything that could damage another person.

7. Letting it start in your heart. Total forgiveness must take place in the heart or it is worthless, for "out of the abundance of the heart the mouth speaks" (MATT. 12:34). If we have not truly forgiven those who hurt us, it will come out—sooner or later. But if it has indeed taken place in the heart, our words will show it. When there is bitterness, it will eventually manifest itself; when there is love, there is "no cause for stumbling" (1 JOHN 2:10).

Because forgiveness takes place in the heart, reconciliation is not a necessary prerequisite. Those who believe they are not required to forgive until their offender has first repented and been reconciled to them are not following Jesus' example on the cross. If He had waited until His enemies felt some guilt or shame for their words and actions, He never would have forgiven them.

8. Relinquishing bitterness. Bitterness is an excessive desire for vengeance that comes from deep resentment. It heads the list of things that grieve the Spirit of God (SEE EPH. 4:30-32). And it is one of the most frequent causes of our missing the grace of God. "[Look] carefully lest anyone fall short of the grace of God; lest any root of bitterness springing up cause trouble, and by this many become defiled" (HEB. 12:15).

We must, therefore, begin to get rid of a bitter and unforgiving spirit; otherwise, the attempt to forgive will fail. Relinquishing bitterness is an open invitation for the Holy Spirit to give you His peace, His joy and the knowledge of His will.

This is extremely important when it comes to the matter of reconciliation. If I have totally forgiven a person who has hurt me, I will have no bitterness, and I should not feel the slightest bit of guilt or shame for not wanting a complete restoration of that relationship.

Even if there never had been a friendship in the first place, if someone has greatly wronged me, I can forgive him and yet see it as totally reasonable not to invite him to lunch every Sunday.

How can we be sure that there is no bitterness left in our hearts? Bitterness is gone when there is no desire to get even or punish the offender, when I do or say nothing that would hurt his reputation or future, and when I truly wish him well in all he seeks to do.

9. Forgiving God. Although we often do not see it at first, all of our bitterness is ultimately traceable to a resentment of God. Why? Because deep in our hearts we believe He is the one who allowed bad things to happen.

Only a fool would claim to know the full answer to the question, "Why does God allow evil and suffering to continue when He has the power to stop it?"

But there is a partial answer: He does so in order that we may believe. There would be no need for faith if we knew the answer about the origin of evil and the reason for suffering. I know only that it is what makes faith possible.

God can turn evil into blessing. He causes things to work together for good. God did not send His Son into the world to explain evil but rather to save us from it and to exemplify a life of suffering. Jesus suffered as no one else has or ever will.

One day God will clear His own name from the charge of being unjust, but in the meantime, we need to trust Him and take Him at His Word that He is just and merciful.

If we will patiently wait for God's purposes to be fulfilled, in the end—this is a guarantee—we will say that He has done all things well, even in what He permitted. He was never guilty in the first place, but because He sometimes appears to us to have been unfair, we must relinquish our bitterness and wholly forgive Him.

10. Forgiving ourselves. There is no lasting joy in forgiveness if it doesn't include forgiving ourselves. It is as wrong as not forgiving others because God loves us just as much as He loves His other children, and He is just as unhappy when we don't forgive ourselves as He is when we hold a grudge against others.

Put simply, we matter to God. He wants our lives to be filled with joy. That's why He commands us to forgive even ourselves.

Total forgiveness brings such joy and satisfaction that I am almost tempted to call it a selfish enterprise. In fact, studies show that the first person to experience delight when forgiveness takes place is the one who forgives.

So, for your own sake, obey God. Let go of your hurts by forgiving—totally—those who have wounded you.

Bio
R.T. Kendall pastored Westminster Chapel in London for 25 years. He is the author of more than 30 books, including The Word and the Spirit, The Sensitivity of the Spirit and Total Forgiveness, all from Charisma House.

3

The Supernatural Power of Forgiveness

Are you holding someone in prison because of your resentment?
Miracles are unleashed when you choose to forgive.

By Mike Fehlauer

Tom and Florence were faithful members of a church in Springfield,
Illinois. Now that their children were out of the house, they were
looking forward to the years they would have together as husband
and wife, doing all the things they had planned. But their dreams
faded instantly one Saturday morning when Tom went to the local
convenience store.

Shortly after Tom entered the store, a man came storming in from
a nearby apartment. It was clear by his expression and the glazed
look in his eyes that he was high on some type of drug. Carrying a
hammer and screaming about the noise from the construction
nearby, he grabbed the nearest person and slammed the hammer
into his skull. Moments later, it was Tom who lay lifeless on the floor.

In the aftermath of this horrible and senseless crime, Florence was
bewildered. Because of a few drug-crazed moments, her life was
drastically changed. Not only was she challenged by the difficulties
that attend losing a mate, she was also challenged by the
Scriptures that deal with forgiveness and mercy—Scriptures such
as Mark 11:25: "'And whenever you stand praying, if you have
anything against anyone, forgive him, that your Father in heaven
may also forgive you your trespasses'" (NKJV).

Nothing reveals the health of our relationship with God more than
how we respond to those who have wronged us. And nothing has
a greater potential to poison our lives and sabotage our future than
how we handle life's offenses.

I receive many phone calls throughout the year from individuals
who are struggling to get beyond offenses. They are living with the
damaging effects of anger and bitterness—emotions that affect
every other relationship they have.

It is not that people don't want to forgive. It's not that they enjoy the emotional roller coaster of anger and resentment. I believe people who struggle with offense are bound by three misconceptions that serve as barriers to a life of forgiveness.

Misconception 1:

Forgiveness Is Simply an Act of the Will

When we are wronged, we are faced with the opportunity to forgive—to release the offender from his wrongdoing. This requires an act of the will, usually in the face of some very real and intense emotions of hurt, disappointment and anger.

But many people believe forgiveness is fully accomplished by this act of the will. We mistakenly assume forgiveness is defined by our decision not to "return evil for evil."

But after we have made the choice to forgive, we must still resolve the disturbing emotions of bitterness, anger, resentment and some-times-even hatred that attend the offense. If we don't, we will experience the dizzying effect of spinning in the revolving door of our emotions, going from forgiveness to unforgiveness more times than we care to admit.

Emotional healing is not the result of our own effort, however; it requires a supernatural work of the Holy Spirit. In Luke 17:4, Jesus says, "'And if he sins against you seven times in a day, and seven times in a day returns to you, saying, "I repent," you shall forgive him.'" The disciples' response to this seemingly impossible command was, "Lord, increase our faith."

In Matthew 18:22, Jesus takes the requirement for forgiveness several steps further, saying that we must forgive "seventy times seven"; that is, always, all the time—no matter how great the offense might be.

This command bankrupts our human resources. To endlessly forgive those who wrong us over and over again literally defies the laws of human nature. It requires a supernatural work of the grace of God to love the offender and walk free from any emotions attached to the wrongdoing.

Jesus told us, "'If you have faith as a mustard seed, you can say to this mulberry tree, "Be pulled up by the roots and be planted in the sea," and it would obey you'" (Luke 17:6). Yet we know it is impossible by natural means to uproot a tree with mere words. Jesus was saying that there is a grace available to us that transcends the laws of nature.

Just as it is impossible in our own strength to uproot a tree by a word, it is impossible to truly forgive. Forgiveness is supernatural! When we place our faith in Jesus, He gives us grace to transcend not only the offense but also all the painful, ugly emotions that torment us.

Misconception 2:

I Am Required to Forgive Only Those Who Ask for Forgiveness

Many come to this conclusion based on the condition stated in Luke 17:4: "'[If he] returns to you, saying, "I repent," you shall forgive him.'" However, the teaching on forgiveness in this verse is not all-inclusive.

When Jesus hung on the cross, He made seven statements, one of which was, "'Father, forgive them, for they do not know what they do'" (Luke 23:34). As far as we can tell from the gospel accounts, not a single person came to Him and repented before Jesus made this statement.

In Ephesians 4:32 we read, "And be kind to one another, tender-hearted, forgiving one another, even as God in Christ forgave you." How were we forgiven? Totally, completely and before we had even sinned!

In fact, we were forgiven by God long before we asked for forgiveness or knew we needed to be forgiven. We must forgive others in like manner. True forgiveness must be based both on our decision and on the work of God established in our hearts—apart from and unaffected by the actions and attitudes of others.

Misconception 3:

Unforgiveness Gives Us Control

When we are wronged, the anger and disappointment that we experience comes from the feeling that we have been betrayed. This often results in the sense that we have lost control of some aspect of our lives to the offender.

Our choice to hold on to the offense is actually an attempt, through our anger, to regain control—like the unforgiving master described in Matthew 18:34: "'And his master was angry, and delivered him to the torturers until he should pay all that was due to him.'"

When we attempt to imprison someone with our unforgiveness, it is actually we who are imprisoned and tormented. We do not regain, but relinquish, control of our hearts and emotions.

If we do not resolve the unforgiveness, we will become victims of what I call "perceived offenses." We will begin to interpret the actions of others as offenses when they actually are not. We will view the decisions and events around us as personal attacks. Our whole perspective relative to our personal relationships will be jaded by our own hurts and disappointments.

It is so important for us to find our security in God's love for us! If we don't, then every relationship we have will be colored by past disappointments. Consequently, we will find ourselves sitting perilously close to the seat of judgment.

The Danger of Judgment

Jesus warns us about the danger of judging others: "'Judge not, that you be not judged. For with what judgment you judge, you will be judged; and with the measure you use, it will be measured back to you.

"'And why do you look at the speck in your brother's eye, but do not consider the plank in your own eye? Or how can you say to your brother, "Let me remove the speck from your eye"; and look, a plank is in your own eye?

"'Hypocrite! First remove the plank from your own eye, and then you will see clearly to remove the speck from your brother's eye. Do not give what is holy to the dogs; nor cast your pearls before swine, lest they trample them under their feet, and turn and tear you in pieces'" (MATT. 7:1-6).

Traditionally, we have interpreted verse six to mean that we should not attempt to witness to those who do not want to hear the gospel. If we do, they will treat our words with contempt and turn on us in some way. Actually, Jesus is still talking here about the danger of sitting in judgment over someone's life.

What He is saying is this: When we judge another, we are throwing the pearl of God's mercy (that which is holy) to Satan, giving him the opportunity to trample what has been covering our transgressions and allowing him to tear our lives to pieces.

Judgment takes us out from under the covering of God's mercy and grace, exposing us to the judgments of Satan against our lives. Satan is merciless and will not think twice about ripping our lives and families apart.

Once again, consider Jesus' words: "'Judge not, that you be not judged. For with what judgment you judge, you will be judged; and with the measure you use, it will be measured back to you'" (MATT. 7:1-2).

Several years ago, a prominent minister felt it necessary to publicly judge another man, and within a year his own private sin was exposed. Unforgiveness is definitely a "door" that we must, by the grace of God, slam shut.

Remember Florence? The man who murdered her husband, Tom, was arrested, tried and convicted. Sometime afterward, Florence visited the man in prison. She stood outside his cell, explaining how he had robbed her of her lifetime mate, their retirement years together and even her financial stability.

Then, handing the man her husband's Bible as a gift, she told him that she forgave him. The killer was so stunned by Florence's act of love that he read the Bible and gave his life to Christ.

I do not know the details of his sentence, but I do know that today this man is out of prison and preaching the gospel. In fact, he returned to Springfield and preached at the church Florence still attends.

It is amazing to me to think of Florence sitting in the congregation, listening to the man who killed her husband tell how he was transformed by the power of God's love through her simple act of obedience. Impossible, you say? Don't tell Florence; she knows the miracle working, transforming power of genuine forgiveness.

Bio
Mike Fehlauer is the director of Foundation Ministries in Colorado Springs, Colorado.

4

Escape from the Performance Trap

By David Morris

The alarm rang sharply at 5:30 a.m. Refusing to be summoned so abruptly, I hit the snooze button and rolled over. Nine minutes later, the alarm's shrill cry was repeated. Again I hit the snooze button. This exhibition of personal discipline, or lack thereof, continued until 6:30 a.m.

Now, with hardly enough time for a quick shower and a cold bagel, I leaped out the door for another challenging day. Unfortunately, this particular morning had become the rule rather than the exception. Day after day the routine continued with the same goal in mind: getting up early for devotions.

I had committed to spending time alone with God before each day began. But it seemed that every time I tried to prove my love for Him by dragging my tired carcass out of bed early, I just could not rouse myself. This serious lack of discipline had become so familiar that I could not summon the energy to change.

All my life I had heard about the importance of personal devotion and private worship. Desiring above all to gain points with God, I knew I must rise to this level of pristine performance if I were to get anywhere in the kingdom.

After all, I thought, grace from God is only available after I've exhausted every other natural resource. I must prove my worth as a lover of God, or He cannot help me. I must endeavor to prove I am a man of God who is after His heart. I must prove...I must prove.

Part of me wanted to bless the Lord with genuine love and faithfulness through this obedient act of a "quiet time." However, the proverbial "flesh-and-spirit" battle was raging within me. I wondered, Will there ever be a decisive victory in favor of the righteous side of me, or will I be held in the grips of this mediocre spiritual life forever?

With tenacity waning, I knew that somehow I had to stop and take some personal stock. I had to ask the hard questions: Why do I do what I do? What's really inside of me, anyway?

My distorted views of Father God were based on years of practice. I rehearsed ways in which I could please the God whom I believed to be an eternally angry potentate. Though I was a Christian from an early age, I believed that perfection was the only acceptable offering.

Proving myself and my love for God was based on nothing but what I thought I should do for Him. Therefore my worship of Him became nothing but a "performance with a smile" on the stage of life. And if others were fooled into believing I was holy, then I too could believe I was.

Still, deep in my heart I knew there had to be more to this private life of devotion. I ached to know the God so many people talked about on a deeply personal level. I longed to hear His voice and be comfortable with Him.

What a grim existence! My faith was built on my ability to perform well for God. I had reduced my relationship with God to the need for approval from spiritual men. This state of idolatry kept me marching to the drumbeat of man rather than resting in the heart-beat of God's love.

I recognized my sinful nature and how large the chasm was between God and me. I thought even the blood of Jesus couldn't span that. The treadmill of performance was the only way to gain acceptance from God and access to His love.

The guilt of sin was a factor, but shame was the real culprit. I was ashamed of who I was. The person I had become with all my serious, hidden faults was not acceptable to me, and I erro-neously believed there was no way I could be acceptable to God—even through Jesus Christ. Self-deception was catapulting me toward disaster.

Drowning in Shame

The gerbil's wheel I was on came to a screeching halt when I fell off, landing in immorality. The pattern of iniquity I had become so familiar with paved an enticing path to destruction. With my limited scope of God's love and the way I operated to please Him, it was only a matter of time before my energy level was depleted. I lost my prover-bial footing, slipped and plunged headlong into the abyss of adultery.

Sometimes when we sin greatly, we are merely attempting to prove that we do not deserve God's love. We unwittingly believe that because we have been rejected and have rejected ourselves, we can out-sin the magnitude of His love. And yet, it is only when we hit bottom that we find God's merciful arms stretched out to catch us.

I never intended to hurt my wife, my children or the church family I belonged to. But the choices I had made, based on my inability to maintain the pace I had set for myself, did a world of damage to those I loved and to those who loved me. The guilt was over-whelming. I couldn't bear to face anyone.

I thought there could be no forgiveness and restoration for me. My sin was much greater than the love of God. The idol of self-suffi-ciency, which I had worshiped for so long, contributed to the length of time it took me to find God again.

Suicide became such a viable option that I soon believed there was no other choice. Fortunately, I had a major emotional collapse before I could do anything too damaging to myself or my family. I now see that experience as God's mercy upon me. Looking up through the bottom of life's darkest dungeon, I realized that if God didn't save me, I would never climb out of the hole I was in, and I would surely die.

I did not want to live without Jesus and His help. But I could not live with Him either, consistently faced with the reality of what I had done.

Then slowly—ever so slowly—the process of God's healing power began to peek over my dismal horizon as I daily chose to give up the ideas of who I thought God was. The aloneness I had experi-enced was the plan of God to reintroduce me to a brand-new concept of life—Jesus.

It took all the years of my growing up in the church, through Bible school and into adulthood and ministry to come face-to-face with a holy God amid the shambles of my life. I had no "props" to support me or any trophies to justify my worth. There was no proving that I had done enough good to merit God's blessing upon me. There I stood, naked and alone before my Maker with nothing to offer Him but all my misunderstandings, bad attitudes, and a lot of pain and fear.

Then, with nothing but brokenness to offer and His mercy to appeal to, I heard Him say, "Ahh, now we can begin again." Instantly, the walls of my performance orientation began to penetrate the darkness of shame's imprisoning walls. Through the valley of the shadow of death, I finally met the real Jesus.

Up to this point, I had lived my life thinking, I am what I do. I was a gifted musician and worship leader, and it was easy to find my identity in those things. From time to time I would revolt against this pigeonhole I found myself in. I wanted to be treated like a person rather than a commodity, but the transition was too great.

But now I saw that even through the darkness that had overtaken my soul, a thread of hope had been woven into the tapestry of my life, bringing a true revelation of His glorious calling. God did have a plan for me in spite of the enemy's designs to destroy the precious seed. And Jesus was literally redeeming my life from the pit, setting me free from the lies that defined me.

That day I began a journey, which I intend to pursue as my life's goal: to consistently acknowledge my utter dependence upon God; to allow myself the luxury of this holy quest; to find His favor outside of my "perfect" performance; and to cultivate an awareness of Him through living life and giving myself to Him. The result? True worship.

Resting in Jesus

True worship flows out of freedom—the freedom to be real before God and, therefore, right with others. For me, that meant admitting my mistakes and humbling myself before my wife and friends. I had to fight my pride, my defensiveness and my desire to blame. I had broken their trust and left a lot of wreckage in my wake.

But because God had met me at the crash site, I now trusted Him to help me pick up the shattered pieces of my life and transform them into a tool for ministry to others. And that is just what He has done. The result is a life that overflows with gratitude that I am forgiven. And such undeserved forgiveness is manifested in praise that is demonstrated in heartfelt worship.

As the years have passed, I've come to believe the responsibility that I assumed by confessing my sin to my wife and the church elders has produced an "on purpose" accountability that is now a comfort rather than a constraint. In submitting to an extended process of restoration, the Lord has truly restored me to my family and to the ministry that He called me to years ago.

Today I want to live and be free to love Him potentially more than yesterday. The pathway of learning that nothing can separate me from the love of God in Christ Jesus has been paved with pain, but it has taken me to a place of grace—the promised land—where life is no longer dependent on my performance but on His undeserved forgiveness and favor. I now live, breathe and find my life in Him.

The ongoing, progressive revelation of God as my loving heavenly Father and His truth caused me to finally find Him and the answers I had searched for all my life. I finally realized the truth that "He who has entered His rest has himself also [rested] from his works" (HEB. 4:10, NKJV). A lifestyle that is pleasing to God is one that finds its rest in Him so that He can do His work in us and eventually through us. Someone has said that we must constantly beware that the work we are doing for God does not interfere with the work He is doing in us.

My time with God in private devotion and worship became very much the same as tending a garden. It took a serious investment of time and energy before the Lord brought permanent change to my life through personal times of devotion.

It became evident to me that just as certain seeds need more time than others to germinate, God's truths have germination times as well. Some truths of God and His character are more easily assimilated than others. More time is necessary for the deeper truths because of the extent of their root systems.

I begged God for the miraculous "zap" that would turn me into the holy, righteous and godly person I desired to be. I asked Him to "grow me up" in a hurry, but He didn't work like that. He used the process of time-developed relationship to show me that His principles of sowing and reaping are both natural and spiritual laws.

I learned that lasting changes happen over life, not overnight. We don't get a life—we cultivate a life. It must cost us something because we must invest in the land to fully appreciate it. Financial investments, job seniority, child rearing and education all fall into this same category. Paying the price includes time, energy and money.

Likewise, there is a cost to the pursuit of holiness that most are unaware of or perhaps unwilling to pay. And many who are willing are looking for the bargain rate. The price of holiness, however, never goes on sale. We who have invested time and energy walking out of a performance-based relationship with God often find it hard to know what to do with the idea of investing in godliness without stepping right back onto "the stage."

Our challenge is to establish the fact in our hearts that the love of God is forever secured and cannot be earned or shaken. But the blessings of God are contingent upon our obedience. If the Lord says, "Seek My face," our response must be, "Your face, Lord, I will seek."

I'm reminded of King David's plan to build an altar to the Lord on the threshing floor. The property was being given to David by the owner, but David would not accept it. He said, "No, but I will surely buy it from you for a price; nor will I offer burnt offerings to the Lord my God with that which costs me nothing" (2 Sam. 24:24). It would seem that David understood the need to "pursue" God by making his search valuable and calculated.

There was something uniquely special about David's ability to express himself. What was it that enabled him to freely and emotionally articulate his praise and worship as well as his pain and fears to God? Could it be the simplicity of an open heart before Him?

Perhaps it was that there was no guile or deceit in David's heart. It seems that he didn't need to prove anything to himself or to others. David did not live for the praise of people—He lived for openness with God. He refused to hide his humanity from God by wrapping himself in a religious cloak.

I can almost hear you saying: "I want a heart like David's—one after God's own heart. But my personality won't permit me to be so emotional. I tend to be more reserved and in control of my feelings. Can I still have that kind of relationship without all the hoopla?"

The answer is yes—when you allow God, who created you, to be your Master. This means that what He desires is what gives you the greatest pleasure.

It's time to open the hidden areas of your life. Let Him know you, warts and all. You cannot shock Him. He sees and knows more about you than you know about yourself.

Get to know Him through His Word. Let the depths of His character touch the roots of your being. Let His unconditional love uproot your shame until your heart is overwhelmed with gratitude— then all that you do will become an act of worship, and your life will become a song of praise.

Bio
David Morris is worship leader at Manna Fellowship in Fayetteville, North Carolina, and author of A Lifestyle of Worship (Renew).

Break Out of The Trap!

Are you performing for God and other people in order to win acceptance and love? Here's how you can escape this spiritual bondage:

1. Pour out your heart to God.

Tell Him about all the times you've blown it. God is not shocked by our imperfections. "For He knows our frame; He remembers that we are dust" (PSALM 103:14, NKJV). Honestly emptying yourself before Him and learning to rely on His grace as the basis of your acceptance will help you break the cycle of shame.

2. Renew your mind.

Stop reading the Bible with the idea that God is mad at you. Read the story of the prodigal son (LUKE 15:11-32), and meditate on the fact that your heavenly Father loves you even when you stray from Him. Recognize that He wants to lavish His love on you in spite of your shortcomings and mistakes.

3. Submit to His surgery.

Ask the Lord to show you areas in your heart where you are being religious and legalistic. Are you trying to prove your love for God by going to church, reading your Bible daily or overcommitting yourself to certain ministry activities? All these things are good, but we must do them from the proper motivation. Ask God to show you any wrong motives in your heart.

4. Get honest with a close friend.

Share your struggle with a prayer partner. If you are hiding secret sins, being vulnerable about them with a trusted friend can bring healing and help develop humility. "Confess your trespasses to one another, and pray for one another, that you may be healed" (JAMES 5:16).

5. Lose yourself in worship.

Transformation happens when we are with the Father. By simply spending time in His presence, and by listening to Him and obeying what He says, the Holy Spirit will produce the character of Christ in us. We can rest while He does the work! He redeems our broken lives, and then He works through us to help others.

5

Don't Crash and Burn

Americans today—including many Christians—are destroying
their lives with stress, unforgiveness and other dangerous emotions.
Here's how you can avoid an emotional breakdown.

By Janet C. Maccaro, Ph.D., C.N.C.

Many believers live in a prison of unresolved emotional issues, not realizing the price they will ultimately be required to pay because of their failure to deal with the poisonous emotions holding them captive. Negative emotions such as anger, envy and bitterness—as well as the mishandling of stress—can destroy one's health and life. Studies have shown, in fact, that anxious thoughts cause our bodies to release chemicals that actually suppress our immune systems.

That is why the Bible tells us to renew our minds and to fix our thoughts on what is true, honorable and right: "Finally, brethren, whatever things are true, whatever things are noble, whatever things are just, whatever things are pure, whatever things are lovely, whatever things are of good report, if there is any virtue and if there is anything praiseworthy—meditate on these things" (PHIL. 4:8, NKJV).

You must consciously monitor your thoughts on a daily basis. When you are first regaining your emotional health, it may take minute-to-minute monitoring until you get control. But the Lord heals today, just as He did in the past: "Jesus Christ is the same yesterday, today, and forever" (HEB. 13:8).

So it follows that we can be healed of our past, be set free in the present, and be all that we can be in the future. In other words: You can become whole, healed and free; you can experience life as God intended it to be.

You must, however, have the willingness and the desire to do so. You must do the work. It will not be easy. It may, in fact, be the most difficult task you have ever undertaken.

Looking deep within yourself takes a lot of courage. But that is where the Holy Spirit comes in and holds you up as you go deep within. With God's help, the process is accelerated. That is why prayer and a close walk with Him are imperative.

In order to appropriately deal with the emotional baggage holding us back, we need to recognize dangerous emotions and understand how they work. And we must make a conscious choice to ban the cluttered thought processes in our minds that lead to stress and breakdown.

Toxic Emotions

The dangerous emotions we must guard against are prolific and include jealousy, pride, envy, anger and bitterness. It is important to understand what plays into each one of these emotions.

Low self-esteem and the absence of unconditional love are often at the root of jealousy. Jealousy is a very destructive emotion because it is self-defeating. You can feel jealous only when you believe someone or something else has or is doing, being or withholding something you desire.

Jealousy is founded on the false idea that God has supplied only a limited amount of love or good in this world. If you believe this, you will become jealous of those who receive more than you do of what you desire. The truth is that God gives you abundance, which is yours just by asking Him in faith.

When you learn to love yourself unconditionally, your self-esteem and confidence become impregnable. You will realize there is nothing to be jealous about. You will be able to accept and love others without fear or envy. "Perfect love casts out fear" (1 John 4:18).

When you see a friend or acquaintance achieve or acquire something wonderful in life, be happy and thankful for them. Any feelings of jealousy will only hurt you and retard your progress.

Pride is another toxic emotion often caused by low self-esteem. Low self-esteem also produces envy, anger, prejudice, resentment and arrogance. These personality traits may be labeled as pride, but in fact they are pride turned inside out. Any exercise in false pride may harm another and always hurts the person misusing his or her proud nature.

False pride is usually born out of fear, self-doubt and anger. The person becomes heavily burdened with fear and self-doubt and angrily rebels against these traits by adopting a superior attitude.

True self-confidence is a healthy mixture of faith, self-control, compassion, achievement, purpose and love. As you learn to see yourself as a child of God, you cannot help but be self-confident of all that you are in Him and all that you are becoming through His help.

Many people struggle with envy, which is typically associated with low self-esteem and an unforgiving, resentful nature. Envy and resentment can keep you trapped in a life that prevents you from God's abundance. The surest way to become poor in spirit and in your pocketbook is to be envious of others.

Envy is an enemy to success in life and causes a multitude of problems, most of them to the person who is envious. Building your self-confidence daily will gradually replace all of the life-destroying effects that envy brings on your mind, body and spirit.

God made you a very special and unique expression of Him. No one else is just like you. You are valuable to God. Therefore, there is no reason for you to be envious of anyone or anything—because you have it all.

One of the most dangerous of all emotions is anger. When anger is not dealt with immediately, it festers in our souls, causing pain, isolation and eventually physical disease. That is why the Bible says not to "let the sun go down on your wrath" (EPH. 4:26).

Warning signs of anger include low self-esteem; an inability to get close to people; being overly critical, controlling or confrontational; lacking in trust; blaming others for mistakes; and overreacting.

An example from nature helps to illustrate the danger of unresolved anger. If a tree is hit with lightning, it may survive unharmed. But it may also suffer damage ranging from minor to severe.

If a rain-drenched tree is hit by lightning, chances are it will not be injured because the moisture on the outside of the tree will conduct the lightning along the outside to the ground. On the other hand, if the tree is dry and has a wet, dead area inside the trunk, it could literally explode—slinging branches and propelling pieces of wood as far as 100 feet. This happens because the lightning travels rapidly down the moist interior of the tree, heating it to a very high temperature in thousandths of a second.

This is a good illustration of the explosiveness of a fiery temper. When you begin to boil inside, harm will come to you. That is why the psalmist said, "Cease from anger, and forsake wrath; do not fret—it only causes harm" (Ps. 37:8). As in the case of the tree blazing inside, "'Wrath kills a foolish man'" (Job 5:2).

The Greek root for the word wrath means "to sacrifice, kill, slaughter." Like lightning traversing the inside of a tree, wrath can boil up inside a person in an instant and even bring about death. Like the tree in which the lightning travels, a person filled with wrath or anger is apt to explode. The Bible puts it this way: "Anger rests in the bosom of fools" (Eccl. 7:9).

If anger is not dealt with, bitterness sets in. You can choose to hold on to your hurt or pain and grow increasingly bitter, or you can deal with it, release it and feel better.

I have a close friend who dramatically illustrates this. He and his sister lived in the same home growing up. Both of them were the products of their parents' divorce. His sister slowly became bitter over the course of her life. She assumed the victim role early on, and the victim she certainly became.

She was an angry child and teen. In adulthood, her anger, resentment and blaming nature paralyzed her life so much that she turned to drugs and alcohol. Although she overcame her drug and alcohol habit, she is still unable to form lasting and meaningful relationships.

The difference for you will be how you choose to react. Long ago I chose to be a survivor. I experienced loss, but I forgave, released and loved. Today I am truly grateful because I am better for it.

The Power of Forgiveness

I have learned that many of our hurts and much of our emotional pain is made worse when we believe that others deliberately wronged us. In some cases, it may be true. But in most cases, people are so busy with their own lives that they simply have no time to purposely cause hurt and pain to others. Much of the emotional pain we experience is unintentionally inflicted upon us.

The path to healing is forgiveness. Forgiveness short-circuits a cascade of stress hormones that can cause accelerated heart rate, shut down your immune system and encourage blood clotting. Conversely, unforgiveness and holding on to anger increase your chance of a heart attack fivefold. They also increase your risk of cancer, high blood pressure, high cholesterol and a host of chronic diseases.

But forgiveness is a conscious choice. You must choose to give up your feelings of unforgiveness and anger. Although anger and resentment are perfectly natural responses to situations that hurt or upset you, it is not worth running the risk of letting negative experiences affect your attitude about people or life in general. If you do, you will be open to emotional health robbers such as anxiety, depression, poor self-esteem and staying in the victim role.

Forgiving is not necessarily forgetting. It is unrealistic to think that you can forget about an injustice, hurt or wound inflicted upon you by someone you love. You do have a memory, and the memory will always be with you.

Forgiving is letting go of the anger and hurt attached to it and moving on with your life. Forgiving results in better sleep, increased feelings of love, more ability to trust and the eradication of physical symptoms that are connected to anger or unforgiveness.

Life is always moving forward; it does not stop and look back. It moves forward at a steady pace, and in doing so, it gives us new opportunities to put into use what was learned from past mistakes. Every day is a new beginning—another chance to live in forgiveness, unconditional love and truth.

The power of love can heal us of the dangerous emotions that threaten to destroy our lives and our health. It is your choice. When you let go of dangerous emotions, you are then free to experience pure love. You will also be able to receive love and give love without fear.

You will experience a peaceful trust that will replace the mistrust that has held you captive. You will feel more relaxed and at peace in your relationships with your friends, family and loved ones. Once you are free to accept and to give love, you will begin to allow this love to flow out of you and into the lives of everyone you come in contact with.

This is actually the way God made us to be. We thrive mentally, physically and spiritually when we develop a lifestyle of loving people unconditionally. Everyone desires love and needs to be loved. You will be amazed at the transformation that takes place in your life. People will be drawn to you.

Love is a balm that produces healing and change. This is because love is unconditional giving. Love is the healing emotion that cancels out all dangerous ones and eliminates fear. Love can set you free from your prison of toxic emotions.

Bio
Janet C. Maccaro, Ph.D., C.N.C., is a nutritionist, lecturer and author. She graduated with doctorates in nutrition and natural healing. Her most recent book is Natural Health Remedies (Siloam Press).

Mastering Your Emotions

Learning what the Bible says about dealing with toxic emotions can put you on the path to overcoming them.

Anger and Bitterness

"A fool vents all his feelings, but a wise man holds them back" (Prov. 29:11, NKJV).

"He who is often rebuked, and hardens his neck, will suddenly be destroyed, and that without remedy" (Prov. 29:1).

"So then, my beloved brethren, let every man be swift to hear, slow to speak, slow to wrath" (James 1:19).

"Pursue peace with all people, and holiness, without which no one will see the Lord: looking carefully lest anyone fall short of the grace of God; lest any root of bitterness springing up cause trouble, and by this many become defiled" (Heb. 12:14-15).

Anxiety

"Be anxious for nothing, but in everything by prayer and supplication, with thanksgiving, let your requests be made known to God; and the peace of God, which surpasses all understanding, will guard your hearts and minds through Christ Jesus" (Phil. 4:6-7).

"Anxiety in the heart of man causes depression, but a good word makes it glad" (Prov. 12:25).

"Casting all your care upon Him, for He cares for you" (1 Pet. 5:7).

"'Come to Me, all you who labor and are heavy laden, and I will give you rest'" (Matt. 11:28).

Fear

"The Lord is my light and my salvation; whom shall I fear? The Lord is the strength of my life; of whom shall I be afraid?" (Ps. 27:1).

"'Are not five sparrows sold for two copper coins? And not one of them is forgotten before God. But the very hairs of your head are all numbered. Do not fear therefore; you are of more value than many sparrows'" (Luke 12:6-7).

"For God has not given us a spirit of fear, but of power and of love and of a sound mind" (2 Tim. 1:7).

"There is no fear in love; but perfect love casts out fear, because fear involves torment. But he who fears has not been made perfect in love" (1 John 4:18).

Unforgiveness

"'Forgive us our debts, as we forgive our debtors'" (MATT. 6:12).
"'For if you forgive men their trespasses, your heavenly Father will also forgive you. But if you do not forgive men their trespasses, neither will your Father forgive your trespasses'" (MATT. 6:14-15).
"Then Peter came to [Jesus] and said, 'Lord, how often shall my brother sin against me, and I forgive him? Up to seven times?' Jesus said to him, 'I do not say to you, up to seven times, but up to seventy times seven'" (MATT. 18:21-22).

6

Come Home to the Father

By Jack Frost

I was born with big ears. As a child, I was teased mercilessly, and until I was 40 years old, I could hardly look in a mirror without feeling depressed.

When my youngest son was born, it was obvious from day one that he had inherited the worst of my physical traits. If anyone ever saw our baby pictures side by side, all they could say was, "My goodness!"

I sent Joshua off to his first day of school, hoping for the best. But it was inevitable. When he got off the school bus at the end of the day, he was sobbing.

"Dad, the kids made fun of me all day long! Everybody laughed at my ears. I never want to go back to school again!"

It was a defining moment in my son's life, and I knew it. I immediately took him in my arms, held him tight and told him how handsome he was.

My response changed his life. He never had to go through the suffering I went through because I took the time to comfort him.

When I faced the taunts of other children, my own father never comforted or protected me. He was not able to express love, security or affirmation when I needed it most, and as a result, I experienced pain and rejection I should never have had to feel.

Fortunately, a revelation of the Father's love for me helped to break the cycle of pain in my own life. But for many adults, unresolved father issues from childhood are often a major cause of emotional pain.

Many Christian psychologists believe that the primary influence on a child's identity is the father-child relationship. When that relationship becomes skewed, children grow up having difficulty relating to other male authority figures. And when they become born again, the issues they have with their earthly fathers often transfer to the new relationship they have with their heavenly Father.

The father issues we have may be unconscious or conscious, but until they are resolved through an experiential revelation of the heavenly Father's love, we will be unable to experience the comforting, affectionate love He has for us. Our anger, fear and distrust, which is often rooted in our hidden pain, easily spills over into every area of our lives—our marriages, our families, our careers, our ministries, our walks with God—and the effects can be devastating.

Father Flaws

All human beings have four basic emotional needs: the need for expressed love, the need to feel secure, the need for praise and affirmation and the need for a purpose in life. As children, we look to our parents, and especially to our fathers, to meet these needs for us.

The family is the place where children learn how to relate to the world, and the lessons learned there are ones carried throughout a lifetime. When these four needs go unmet in childhood, it becomes very difficult for a person to develop healthy relationships, with God or with other people, later in adulthood.

Children look to their fathers to meet the four emotional needs, but unfortunately, no earthly father is perfect. Even the best of them fail to meet all their children's needs all the time.

At some point, disappointments, hurts and wounds will inevitably take place, and these cause what I call "father flaws" to form in the hearts of our children. The leftover pain and wounds from childhood create a lens through which adults later view the world.

Most earthly fathers will fall into one of six categories, each of which creates a different home environment for the children. As you read through the six types of fathers, think back to your own childhood and try to determine how your earthly father related to you.

Each type of father creates different father issues in the adult children and different hindrances to an intimate relationship with God. Ask the Holy Spirit to reveal to you any unresolved hidden issues you may still have with your own earthly father that are affecting your ability to relate to your heavenly Father and receive His affectionate love.

The good father. When thinking back to their childhoods, many Christians argue that they came from "good homes" with fathers who loved them and provided for their needs. However, there is no perfect earthly father, and it is impossible for any dad, no matter how good his intentions may be, to raise a child without creating any father issues whatsoever.

Good fathers are just that: good fathers. They provide for their children physically, making sure they have a roof over their heads, clothes to wear and food to eat; and emotionally, they spend time with them and meet their needs for security and affirmation. It seems that children raised in such homes would grow up without any negative repercussions in their adult lives.

But the issues these children have as adults are often very subtle. Sometimes they are unable to let go of their relationships with their earthly dads sufficiently to develop strong relationships with God. Some of these children may even become pastors or ministers because, having become overly attached to their earthly fathers, they are unable to develop an intimate relationship with God and substitute serving Him for intimacy.

The bond between a good father and his child may become an unhealthy dependence later in life if the adult child continues to look to the father for his or her ultimate source of love and security. Daughters, for example, may experience difficulty "leaving and cleaving" when the time comes for them to leave their fathers' homes and become wives to their husbands.

Other times, situations may arise that prevent the father from keeping a promise or meeting one of his child's needs. Even the most well-meaning good father cannot control every situation in his children's lives. This may end up being even more of a disappointment if the children have grown to have unrealistic expectations of their father.

The performance-oriented father. The performance-oriented father is very common in America today because, as a whole, our society rewards individuals who perform successfully, whether it be in sports, careers, academics or the financial market. This father often proclaims that he loves you, but that love is expressed only when you have measured up to his rigid expectations.

Stringent demands for perfect obedience and high-performance standards, if not tempered with large amounts of expressed love, affirmation and praise, often result in many problems later in life. One of these problems is depression.

No one can do everything right all the time because we are only human beings, and we all experience failure. But after 20 or 30 years of striving for perfection, fear and depression can begin to creep into the heart of adult sons and daughters.

Even if they are born again and Spirit-filled, they may still believe that God will be pleased with them only when they have read the Bible enough or prayed at least an hour a day. Eventually, if the pattern continues, they can collapse into burnout, unable to hear God's voice or feel His presence at all.

Boundaries and standards are good, and fathers should encourage their children to be the best they can be. But when expressed love and approval become tied to how well a child performs, problems may result. Any criticism or demands for performance must be tempered with large amounts of affection and affirmation.

The passive father. The passive father does not either make great demands on his children or overtly reject them. He simply fails to be "home" even when he is home. He is unable to demonstrate any sort of love or affection at all, usually because he never received these things from his own father.

He doesn't speak the words of love that his children need to hear; he doesn't reach out to his sons and daughters with warmth or hugs or kisses, or cuddle them on his lap. He may be physically present in the home, but he isn't able to allow himself to be known.

He does not share his joys, his hopes, his sorrows or his disappointments with his wife or children. He does not experience life with his family; he simply lives his life under the same roof.

When a person has been raised in the home of a passive father, his relationship with God may be devoid of passion and joy. Discipline, form and duty keep things safe because he has become uncomfortable with any show of emotion. When relating to God, he often will have a mental or intellectual assent to the gospel but will rarely let the Father touch his heart so that he can truly taste His love.

People like this are quite often the adults who are the quickest to criticize any "emotional" move of the Holy Spirit in the church. Any weeping or loud rejoicing or praise to the Father causes them to feel extremely uncomfortable.

But walking in the Spirit should be an emotional encounter. It's about love, joy and peace much more than it is about the study of doctrine or theory. God wants to touch our hearts and emotions; He wants to restore healthy emotions in our relationships.

The absentee father. Today in America the absentee father is becoming more and more common. He is the one who is no longer physically present in the home due to death, divorce or abandonment.

Fifty percent of children in America wake up each morning with someone other than their natural birth father in the home. And too often this father figure does not have a strong interest in meeting their emotional needs. This is not true in every case, of course; there are godly stepfathers who love their stepchildren as if they were their own, but that is a rare occurrence.

Children who have had an absentee father may face abandonment issues, and it may be very difficult for them to relate to God. Even if they do foster a relationship with Him, there may be a sense of fear that at some point, He will not be there for them. These children need an experiential revelation of God's presence and unconditional love in their lives.

The authoritarian father. Authoritarian fathers are those fathers who are more interested in the love of law than in the law of love. They go beyond the performance-oriented fathers and sternly demand immediate, unquestioned obedience from their children. They foster no positive emotional relationship between themselves and their children; rather, they use intimidation and fear to control them.

These fathers are usually very selfish; the entire life of the family revolves around them and their needs. They do not recognize the unique individuality of each child but see the children as a means to getting their own needs met.

Children raised in such homes will see God as the Great Cop in the sky, a harsh authoritarian figure to be feared and obeyed rather than a loving Father to be enjoyed and cherished. They strive so hard to meet His requirements that they feel more like servants than children whom the Father loves.

The abusive father. Verbal, emotional, physical or sexual abuse is never an acceptable form of behavior for a father to practice. Tragically, however, all these types of abuse are becoming common in families throughout the United States. If you have been abused in any of these ways, you may need more than counseling or psychological therapy to be free from the deep pain and anger; you may need deep healing that can come only as the Holy Spirit pours the love of God into your heart (SEE ROM. 5:5).

Abuse, especially sexual abuse, creates one of the deepest wounds a child can ever experience, for it results in tremendous hidden pain. It violates the trust the child has placed in authority and can affect all his relationships for the rest of his life.

Sexual abuse leaves children consumed with hidden fears and a deep distrust of God, pastors, other authority figures and other men. It creates feelings of guilt and a profound sense of shame and unworthiness.

It can leave children feeling as if they did something to deserve to be treated so badly. And underneath it all, there is tremendous repressed anger, much of it focused on God for allowing the abuse to occur.

No matter what type of father you had as a child, you don't have to remain wounded, carrying the pain from father issues in your heart.

You can forgive your father for each area in which he failed to represent the father-heart of God, and you can release the wounds caused by him to the One who can heal them. You can get to know your heavenly Father through Jesus, who gave His life for us and shows us what His Father is like.

Jesus is always reaching out to pour His love upon us. Allow that perfect love to comfort you as you listen to the words your Father speaks to you, His beloved son or daughter: "My child, I want to rejoice over you with singing. I want to quiet you in My love.

"I have loved you with an everlasting love, and I am drawing you with lovingkindness. I will not leave you as an orphan, but I will come to you and bless you as My child" (SEE ZEPH. 3:17; JER. 31:3; JOHN 14:18,21).

Whatever needs you have—physical, spiritual or emotional—your heavenly Father can fill them as no earthly father ever could. Come home to Him, and give Him the opportunity to show you how loving, dependable and constant He is.

Bio
Jack Frost and his wife, Trisha, direct Shiloh Place Ministries in Conway, South Carolina.

7

The Faith of George W. Bush

Not all Christians like George W. Bush's politics. But most agree
that he discovered faith in Christ the old-fashioned way.

By Stephen Mansfield

Men come to faith in many ways. Some have dramatic experiences
that fill them with certainty. Some cling to their parents' God from
childhood. Others live through gut-wrenching cycles of doubt and
belief until the latter triumphs.

Still others arrive at faith through a long process, as though a
temple of the heart is being readied for a destined moment. This
is how faith came for George W. Bush.

By the time he turned 40, Bush had been churched. He was
baptized in an Episcopal church in Connecticut, trained for a decade
in the First Presbyterian Church of Midland, Texas, and made to feel
stirrings of faith in St. Martin's Episcopal Church of Houston.

During his high school years at Phillips Academy in Massachusetts,
he was required to be in a Congregationalist-style chapel five times
a week, which meant he spent as much time in church in those
three years as a regular attendee does in 10.

After he got to Yale, he began taking religion in smaller doses.
Perhaps he needed a break.

It was his wife, Laura, who drew him in again and made him a
Methodist. Not long after their marriage, he was teaching Sunday
school at First Methodist in Midland, taking up offerings and sitting
on committees. Whether his heart was engaged by it or not, he
had known since childhood that a good man stays connected to
his faith.

A friend once remarked that if Bush had stopped going to church
at the age of 40 he would still have attended more than most
people do in a lifetime.

But, again, Bush was bored by the time he arrived at midlife. Laura took him to a James Dobson seminar in hopes of seeing him deepen spiritually.

It didn't take. George got up from his seat and moved next to a friend. The quips began. "What kind of pants did the Levites wear?" he whispered.

Another time, a pastor asked, "What is a prophet?" Bush sang out: "That is when revenues exceed expenditures. No one's seen that out here in years."

Bush relished being the bad boy. He once set the timer on his watch to go off in the middle of a pastor's talk to a men's class. Everyone but the pastor thought it was hilarious, and the next week all the men set their watches to go off at the same time.

By 1984, though, events conspired to help him concentrate. Oil prices started collapsing. Life in Midland changed dramatically.

The big spending came to a neck-snapping halt, and the town in which 1 in every 45 citizens had been a millionaire began to see foreclosures, bankruptcy and fear. Bush's small firm lost more than $400,000, and there were more hits to come.

The economy was but one force driving Bush into confrontation with himself. To top it all off, he had never shaken his chief demon: the aimlessness, the lack of purpose, the boredom that had plagued him all his life.

He had no sense of destiny. He could party and do business and love his family, but he did not have the inner fire that makes men happy and great. He was a lightweight in almost every sense.

The story of Bush's spiritual transformation has usually centered upon his famous walk on a Maine beach with Billy Graham. Bush has said that Graham "planted a mustard seed in my soul," but if this is so, it happened only after a year of deep plowing by others.

An Encounter With the Cross

In 1984, the spiritual leaders of Midland were trying to tend the souls of a troubled community. To bring the needed healing, the city's religious leaders invited the people of Midland-Odessa to gather at the Chaparral Center during the first week of April to hear famed evangelist Arthur Blessitt—the man who had carried a 12-foot cross some 38,800 miles in 284 nations.

Billed as Decision '84, Blessitt's meetings in Midland were widely advertised on radio and television. Several days into the meetings, on April 3, Blessitt received a call from Jim Sale, an oilman, Baptist church member and one of the organizers of the crusade. Sale told Blessitt that there was another local oilman who had heard the radio advertising and wanted to meet him.

But this was no ordinary oilman, Sale explained. This was George W. Bush, son of the vice president of the United States.

Blessitt agreed to see him, and the three met that day in the coffee shop of Midland's Holiday Inn. After a brief exchange of greetings, Bush looked at Blessitt and said, "Arthur, I did not feel comfortable attending the meeting, but I want to talk to you about how to know Jesus Christ and how to follow Him."

The evangelist reflected for a moment and asked, "What is your relationship with Jesus?"

"I'm not sure," Bush replied.

Blessitt probed. "If you died this moment do you have the assurance you would go to heaven?"

Bush did not hesitate. "No," he answered.

The evangelist then began to explain what it meant to know and follow Jesus. He quoted the Bible, verse after verse, commenting as he went, and making application to Bush's life. After he had outlined the Christian message, he said: "The call of Jesus is for us to repent and believe. The choice is like this: Would you rather live with Jesus in your life or live without Him?"

"With Him," Bush replied.

"Jesus changes us from the inside out," Blessitt continued. "The world tries to change us from the outside in. Jesus is not condemning you. He wants to save you and cleanse your heart and change your desires. He wants to write your name in the Book of Life and welcome you into His family, now and forever."

Blessitt then asked Sale to share his testimony, believing that Bush would relate to the story of a fellow oilman. When Sale was done, Blessitt said: "Mr. Bush, I would like to pray a prayer for you and then lead you in a prayer of commitment and salvation. You can become a follower of Jesus now."

Bush had some questions, though, and the two men took time to answer each one until he seemed satisfied.

The evangelist pressed again: "I want to pray with you now."

"I'd like that," Bush said.

Blessitt then prayed, asking Bush to repeat each phrase after him. When the prayer ended, Bush was smiling, and Blessitt began rejoicing. It was an "an awesome and glorious moment," the evangelist recalls.

Blessitt read Luke 15:10 to Bush, which says there is joy in the presence of God's angels over one sinner who repents. He then gave Bush a pamphlet titled The New Life, which explained how to grow as a young Christian. After a few more pleasantries, the two shook hands and parted.

Over the next two years, they spoke by phone several times, but Blessitt's long seasons of travel abroad caused them to lose contact.

Sale and Blessitt kept silent about the meeting for 17 years. They assumed it was private and not for them to speak publicly of Bush's spiritual life. When A Charge to Keep was published in 2001, with Bush so strongly writing about his faith in its pages, Blessitt decided it was appropriate for him to begin telling of the meeting in Midland. He published his recollection on his Web site and has often spoken in his sermons of the prayer with Bush.

Sale, the only eyewitness, confirms that "what happened is precisely as recorded in Blessitt's testimony." Indeed, Sale adds that given the 17 years Blessitt went without "saying a word, there is real humility and integrity here that bears witness to the authenticity of the testimony."

Deeper Conviction

For Bush, the encounter with Blessitt was but one in a series of events in those years that pressed the message he had known since childhood even more deeply into his heart. More revealing is how intensely Bush was searching out matters of the Spirit.

He obviously felt so uncomfortable with evangelistic meetings that he couldn't bring himself to attend the one in Midland. He was so moved by what he heard Blessitt say on the radio that he sought a meeting with the man to ask him how to follow Jesus. Clearly Bush was hungry for something he had yet to find in all of his religious experience.

Yet the meeting with Blessitt did not bring Bush's search to an end. When Billy Graham asked him a year later if he was right with God, he answered, "No."

If Bush was hungry, the conversion of his friend Don Jones, the president of Midland's fastest-growing bank, was about to make him hungrier.

Bush knew Jones well. He was on the board of Jones' bank, and the two often drank together. Jones had often joked that he was "raised Episcopalian, and where you find four Episcopalians you'll usually find a fifth."

They also attended First Methodist Church together. For Jones the Episcopalian, the choice of a Methodist church was a compromise with his Southern Baptist wife.

Not unlike his friends at the time, Jones had a low opinion of the "born again" variety of Christians. He thought of them as flashy tele-vangelists with overdone jewelry and side-showman suits: "I sure didn't want to be one," he laughs.

But a sense of moral neediness and some of the spiritual happenings in Midland led Jones in 1985 to make a New Year's resolution to give up drinking and start reading the Bible. It was while home alone on January 10 that he was reading the Gospel of John and came upon the words, "'Unless a man is born again, he shall not see the kingdom of God.'"

Immediately, an overwhelming sense of conviction and need for God's grace came over him. There were tears and a crushing sense of his sinfulness. He prayed and cried and prayed some more. By evening, he felt peace, a sense that "the burden of his sins had been lifted from his soul."

His wife came home to find a different man. Jones developed a virtual addiction to the Bible. He got even more involved in his church and, in November, he started attending Community Bible Study, the Midland branch of a Bible-study movement started in Washington, D.C. The change in him was immediately evident to everyone who knew him, including Bush.

Jones gave his testimony wherever he was invited, and soon nearly all of Midland knew that the prominent banker had been "born again." That Jones was a respected businessman and that he had such a pleasant way of talking about his faith made him easy for men like George Bush to relate to. Still cautious, however, they watched Jones closely over the months and in time decided that the change in his life was real.

It was just as Bush was marveling at Jones' transformation that the famous walk on the beach with Billy Graham took place. In the summer of 1985, the Bush clan vacationed together at Kennebunkport in Maine. Graham joined them for a weekend and preached at the small summer church, St. Ann's by the Sea.

Bush remembers that his father asked Graham to answer questions from a big group of family gathered for the weekend. As Bush told Skip Hollingsworth of *Texas Monthly*: "It was this beautiful Maine night and Billy just sat there and talked to us, and we asked him questions and shared our thoughts. He and I had a visit afterward—it was just a real personal religious visit—and I started reading the Bible."

The "visit afterward" was a walk that Graham and Bush took at Walker's Point the next day. During the conversation, Graham turned to Bush and said, "Are you right with God?"

"No," Bush replied, "but I want to be."

It is typical of Bush that he remembers how he felt being with Graham rather than much of what he said. "I knew I was in the presence of a great man," he recalled in his biography, *A Charge to Keep*. "Billy Graham didn't make you feel guilty; he made you feel loved."

The weekend changed him. "Reverend Graham planted a mustard seed in my soul," Bush later wrote of those few days, "a seed that grew over the next year. I had always been a religious person, had regularly attended church, even taught Sunday school and served as an altar boy.

"But that weekend my faith took on new meaning. It was the beginning of a new walk where I would recommit my heart to Jesus Christ. I was humbled to learn that God sent His Son to die for a sinner like me."

He must have shared something of his experience with his family because sometime later he overhead his mother, Barbara, talking to someone on the phone and saying: "I've got some exciting news. George has been born again."

New Convictions

When he returned to Midland, he found himself possessed by a new hunger for the Bible. His friend Don Evans gave him a Bible with daily readings from both Testaments, Psalms and Proverbs, organized for every day of the year.

He also joined the Community Bible Study that Jones was part of. The group had begun meeting the year before, around the time of the Blessitt meetings. By the time Bush joined, in the fall of 1985, almost 120 men were gathering to study the New Testament writings of Luke.

It is possible that Bush did not fully understand the enormity of what he had joined. The Community Bible Study (CBS) ministry began in 1975 with a group of women who wanted to see "effective" Bible studies serving the Washington, D.C., area. The first class began at Fourth Presbyterian Church in Bethesda, Maryland, with more than 500 women gathering to study the Gospel of John.

The leader was Lee Campbell, who had been deeply influenced in her faith by Christian theologian-historian Francis Schaeffer. The curriculum involved a verse-by-verse study of each book of the Bible. Students were required to spend several hours outside of class, answering questions, meditating on the verses and even turning the words to prayer.

CBS became wildly popular. Within four years, there were classes in 10 states and London. Eventually, there were 19 classes in the Washington area alone. But it wasn't just growth that distinguished

CBS. It was influence. Early participants included Jack Kemp's wife, Joanne; Jim Baker's wife, Donna; and Elizabeth Dole.

As the movement's own literature explains, "The studies had an impact in shaping the thinking of key players in the Reagan Revolution of the eighties." Though nonpolitical and nondenominational, CBS often provided the biblical content that educational programs of local churches lacked.

This was certainly the case for Bush, who found himself now challenged to explore Scripture in a manner he never had before. Every week Jones would drive Bush to the Bible study and marvel at his growth. The truths he was learning and pressing into his heart through prayer and meditation were clearly changing him.

There was a new gravity and maturity in Bush. George the lightweight was becoming a man of serious faith.

Christian theology teaches that salvation is instant, but sanctification—the process of cleaning up a believer's conduct and thinking—takes time. For Bush, a man of habit and routine, the renewing of his life wasn't going to be easy.

"It was like a long struggle up a steep hill for George," Jones says. It would take years for some habits to go. His tendency to strong language, for example, would die-hard. Yet, his famed struggle with alcohol ended quickly, and it says much about the man he was becoming.

Bush has joked that he is so cheap he only stopped drinking when he saw the bar bill. The truth is that his moral compass and sense of values were being reconfigured by his deepening faith. He knew of Jones' decision to stop drinking and the good that it had done in his life. Still, getting drunk was the sin, not drinking alcohol, and he saw no reason to stop completely.

The change in his thinking came just after his 40th birthday. The Bushes joined their friends the O'Neills and the Evanses for a trip to the Broadmoor Hotel in Colorado Springs, Colorado.

After the night of drinking at the Broadmoor, he went for a run, assuming exercise would help overcome the effects of alcohol. It didn't.

Bush wrote: "For the past fourteen years, I had run at least three miles almost every day. This run was different. I felt worse than usual, and about halfway through, I decided I would drink no more. I came back to the hotel room and told Laura I was through."

The decision to quit alcohol is a major turn in Bush's life. It reveals more than what he felt about his health or his father's campaign. It reveals the kind of man that faith was making him. Whether he quit because he found it something he couldn't control or so he wouldn't embarrass his father, the all-important point is that he disciplined himself to serve a cause greater than himself.

He had been arrested for drunkenness, and it hadn't stopped him. His wife had asked him to stop, and he hadn't. He even had made a fool of himself socially on more than one occasion. That hadn't worked either.

But after he had come to faith, he found both the purpose and the discipline to do something that nothing else in his life could induce him to do: sacrifice pleasure on the altar of a greater cause. This new discipline, fueled by a growing sense of purpose, was beginning to make him an exceptional man.

It is also important to note the way Bush stopped drinking. The New York Times said he did it in "a characteristic way: decisively, impulsively and without much evident introspection." This would increasingly become a theme of both his personal life and his brand of leadership. When he recovered his inner moral compass and understood its signals, he obeyed it by doing what he thought was "the right thing."

Certainly he was flawed and would at times choose unwisely. Still, Bush the man without purpose was passing from the scene. In time—and it would take torturous steps over the course of years—he would become Bush the man with a charge to keep.

Bio
Stephen Mansfield grew up primarily in Europe as the son of a U.S. Army officer, an experience that gave him an early love for history and international affairs. He is the author of numerous books on history and leadership, including Never Give In: The Extraordinary Character of Winston Churchill (Cumberland House). He lives in Nashville, Tennessee, and directs the Mansfield Group, a publishing and research firm.

Hope

In the Lord

⠀⠀⠀

"Therefore my heart is glad,
and my glory rejoices;
My flesh also will rest in hope."

Psalm 16:9 NKJV

8

How Desperate Are You for God?

Revival isn't a game of chance. There are specific conditions that must be met if you want to experience a visitation of the Holy Spirit.

By Tommy Tenney

Charles Dickens opened his famous book *A Tale of Two Cities* with the statement, "It was the best of times—it was the worst of times." He was referring to the period of history immediately preceding and including the French Revolution. But his statement is equally applicable to the current day. In many ways, it is both the "best of times" and the "worst of times" for the body of Christ.

Why do I say this? Because some churches are experiencing tremendous growth and a tangible sense of God's presence, while others are experiencing a decline in attendance and an absence of awesomeness.

It is not always possible to determine why God brings revival in one place and not another. We can't definitively predict His movement any more than we can accurately predict the movement of the wind. But we can observe where the wind has blown hard and often before, and then plant ourselves in a likely place.

In doing so, we must be aware that God's logic is often in conflict with man's reasoning. That's because His perspective, unlike ours, is eternal.

To see what I mean, try this experiment: Compare God's assessment of the cities of Nazareth and Nineveh with your own. Because of their reputations, you probably think of Nazareth as a "good" city and Nineveh as a "bad" city. Yet God chose to bless Nineveh with citywide renewal and to allow Nazareth—hometown of the world's greatest preacher—to experience nothing!

What would motivate God to send great revival to Nineveh? After all, the city had a reluctant prophet spewed up by a fish for an evangelist. Nazareth, on the other hand, had Jesus. Looking more closely at these two cities may provide an indication of why one was ripe for a move of God and one wasn't—and why some of our churches today may be more likely to receive the fire of God than others.

A Tale of Two Cities

From an earthly perspective, Nazareth—the "Bible Belt" of the Holy Land in ancient times—had a lot going for it. Jesus grew up there; in fact, He spent more time in Nazareth—30 years—than in any other city on Earth.

Thirty years was certainly ample time for a great revival to occur. In many of the other towns where Jesus ministered, revival took place after only two or three days.

But instead of the setting for great revival, Nazareth was the scene of great rejection. The people Jesus grew up with drove Him out of town—and sought to kill Him. He had to miraculously walk through the crowd in order to keep from losing His life (SEE LUKE 4:28-30).

What could Jesus have said to have provoked such a hostile response? Surely He must have insulted them, preached a harsh message—real fire-and-brimstone stuff. But that wasn't the case at all. Jesus simply read from the book of Isaiah.

He told the people, "The Spirit of the Lord is upon Me, for He has anointed me to preach the gospel to the poor, to heal, to open blind eyes, to set the captives free" (SEE LUKE 4:18). He was telling them what He had come to do, what He wanted to do for them. They could have had it all, but their unbelief shut Him down cold.

The people of Nazareth were haughty and arrogant; they thought they knew Jesus. They thought they knew His family tree. "Isn't this the carpenter's son?" they asked themselves. "Are not His sisters and brothers here with us?"

The truth is, they knew the earthly facts about Jesus, but they didn't know Him. Their false familiarity birthed foolish assumptions. As a result, they did not believe He could do what He said, and they stopped God from moving in their midst.

The city of Nineveh, unlike Nazareth, did not have a lot going for it. It was involved in constant war with Israel and was famous for its atrocities. The people were cruel and heartless—and proud of it!

Often when they would conquer another city, they would capture the men, nail them to trees and disembowel them with a special curved sword. Then they would leave the mutilated bodies hanging there and threaten to kill anyone who would try to take the bodies down. Sometimes they would cut off the heads of their captives and stack them up as a sort of morbid monument.

The city was also large for its day: Its inner walls were eight miles long, and it had a population of more than 120,000 (SEE JOHN. 4:11). Can you imagine Jonah's fear when God called him to go preach there?

The Lord said to Jonah, "'Arise, go to Nineveh, that great city, and cry out against it; for their wickedness has come up before Me'" (JON. 1:2, NKJV). Basically, He was saying: "Here's what I want you to do. Go to that city that disembowels people and tell them: 'You city of sinners! You're in trouble with God. You'd better repent. You'd better quit doing what you're doing because God doesn't like it.'"

Is it surprising that when Jonah heard this command, he got on a ship and went the other way? Jonah was scared. But God knew something he didn't: The people of Nineveh had soft hearts hidden beneath their tough exteriors. If God could just send someone to them who had a greater fear of God than he did of man, revival would break out.

And that is exactly what happened. God interrupted Jonah's escape plan by sending a whale to swallow him and then burp him up on a beach. Jonah didn't want to be there. But after three days in the whale's belly, he was more concerned about the hand of God than he was about the people of Nineveh.

He walked into the city and, in obedience to God, began to cry out against them, warning them of God's impending judgment. History tells us that he walked through the city from one end to the other, and wherever he walked there was a wave of revival: Ahead of him the people were arrogant, but behind him they were repenting.

His basic message was, "Repent, or God is going to destroy you." It wasn't the sort of sermon that would make you popular. And it wasn't one Jonah wanted to preach. He had no desire for Nineveh or its citizens to be saved—in fact, he was hoping God would kill them.

Nevertheless, he performed the task God had given him as quickly as possible and left. No extensive planning, no years of preparation leading to a pivotal moment. An unwilling messenger, a strong message and a tough city: not what we would call a proper equation for revival.

But when Jonah preached "repent or perish," they all fell on their faces. The king declared a fast—one that extended even to the animals—to see if God would have mercy on them. As a result, great revival fell on that city.

The Conditions for Revival

The examples of Nazareth and Nineveh are convincing proof that there are reasons God moves in certain places and doesn't move in other places. There are reasons He is either present or absent in our daily lives.

We can't just say, "Well, sometimes He visits, and sometimes He doesn't." We need to permanently relinquish the "gambler's concept" that revival is hit-or-miss—maybe we'll get it, maybe we won't. Revival is very predictable as long as the conditions are met.

The Bible has an equation for how to bring the presence of God daily into our lives, our churches and our homes. God promises, "If My people who are called by My name will humble themselves, and pray and seek My face, and turn from their wicked ways, then I will hear from heaven, and will forgive their sin and heal their land" (2 Chr. 7:14). Humility plus prayer plus repentance—which are all the result of faith and hunger for God—equals revival.

The reason revival seems unpredictable to us is that we don't see what God sees. We look at the things that seem significant to us and fail to see the things that are significant to God. Often, the places where we think God can move most easily are actually the places where He finds the greatest resistance.

Perhaps we can more adequately assess the potential for revival if we use these three principles as a determining factor:

1. God is more disposed to move on admitted emptiness (a sign of humility) than on presumed fullness. It is easier for Him to "break out" in a church that admits its emptiness than for Him to "break through" in a church that presumes its fullness. The former is aware of its need for Him; the latter is satisfied with what it has.

The people of Nazareth thought they had all they needed. They were so full of themselves, they left no room for a Messiah in their midst. We are sometimes like this.

We can get so full of religious junk food we have no appetite for God, so full of ourselves we become a monument to longevity rather than energy. Proof that once fresh fire can fossilize! You could say we are saved, sanctified and petrified.

But people who are bad and know they're bad and are proud of the fact that they're bad, and who are confronted with the goodness of God, often respond with repentance and change. That's what happened in Nineveh. Their admitted emptiness cracked open the heavens for the rain of revival.

We become like the citizens of Nazareth when we choose to believe that we are pious and righteous enough, that we've got it all together. When we think our goodness is good enough for His righteousness, we leave no room for change.

We need to acknowledge that our righteousness stinks in God's nostrils! We'll never be good enough for God. That's a hard word for most of us; we don't like to hear about our faults, and we don't really want to admit to having any.

But when we acknowledge we've done wrong and openly admit it—that's when God can move! That's when we can be like the citizens of Nineveh and have the kind of revival that Nineveh experienced.

Who can prevent God from moving? Not the drug dealers or the prostitutes or the criminals, but those of us who sit around in self-righteousness thinking we've got it all conquered and understand everything.

God is looking for humble people who will lay themselves on the altar and realize: "I am not good enough, but God has grace enough! Wherever, whenever, however, whomever—I'm ready to go." Jonah went somewhere he didn't want to go, to preach something he didn't want to preach, to people he didn't even like—and had the biggest revival history has ever recorded. That should give us hope!

2. Faith and hunger can hasten a move of God. The opposite is also true: Unbelief and complacency, or self-satisfaction, can hinder it.

The people of Nazareth had unbelief. They were presented with the truth by Jesus Himself but did not believe it because of their familiarity with Him. They thought they had Him figured out.

Like the inhabitants of Nazareth, we think we know God. We think we know what He wants to do, but we really have no idea. We know what it's like when God visits a church. We've seen that model on a limited scale.

But we've not yet seen what it's like when God visits a city. We don't know what it's like when the glory of God sweeps through a city and mows people down left and right, causing them to fall on their faces on the street corners, in the malls, in the hospitals, in the cafeterias, crying out for God. We don't have the faintest idea what that kind of move of God is all about, and as a result we limit what God can do through our unbelief.

We ask ourselves: Whom is God going to visit? Where will He show up? We need to see that it is sometimes easier for God to redeem a drug dealer, an alcoholic or a prostitute and use him rather than to recycle "Christians." It is often easier for Him to convert one of them and set him on fire and use him to change the world than to get one of us, who is sitting on the pews of the church, to do what He really wants.

Familiarity has bred contempt. "He's just Mary's boy." Sacred things have become common. We demand "Uzziah"-friendly services, so God has no choice but to leave us "arkless" (SEE 2 CHR. 26). There is an absence of awesomeness among us. Like Nazareth, we have no revival—false familiarity leads to unbelief and blinds us to the visitation.

If Nazareth had unbelief, Nineveh had misbelief—wrong belief. God can deal much more easily with misbelief. One encounter with Him can transform it into fiery faith in Him. If the New Age advocates ever have a Damascus Road encounter, they will burn up heaven's toll-free lines just as they've flooded the pay-per-call pseudo-psychic hot lines.

How many encounters does the church need to have before unbelief turns into faith and rekindles the dying embers of our first love?

3. Repentance ranks higher in heaven than reputation. In spite of the fact that Nazareth was the boyhood home of Jesus, God's divine Son and the Messiah, it was Nineveh that God called a "great city" (SEE JOHN. 1:2). Obviously, He wasn't using the same measuring stick we do. Future potential is more important to Him than past history. Nazareth had a great history, but Nineveh had a great future.

The difference between Nineveh and Nazareth, and between revival and no revival, is repentance that comes from hunger and humility. Nineveh repented while Nazareth refused to relent. I don't know how to paint a more dramatic picture of the opportunity for revival—or a missed moment.

Jesus Himself preached revival in Nazareth's synagogues, but His message was a total flop. He could do no mighty work in Nazareth at all except "lay His hands on a few sick people and heal them" (MARK 6:5, NIV). That's not much considering what He was capable of doing. But the people did not see their need and were unwilling to repent.

Jonah, on the other hand, walked into one of the worst cities of the world and preached repentance, and a great revival broke out.

What does this tell us? Some churches would not have revival even if Jesus were the evangelist, while others could be set aflame by a few passing words from a reluctant prophet!

Revival in our churches and cities has nothing to do with who does the preaching or who sings. The fires of revival ignite when the spark of God lands in the dry tinderbox of hungry, open hearts marked by true repentance.

So which do you choose, Nazareth or Nineveh? As for me and my house, we're moving to Nineveh, home of the hungry!

Bio
Tommy Tenney is the founder of the GodChasers Network. He has spent 10 years pastoring and 17 years in full-time traveling ministry. He is also the author of The God Chasers (Destiny Image), God's Dream Team (Regal Books) and God's Favorite House (Destiny Image).

9

Don't Let Them Perish

Would you live your life differently if you realized that every non-Christian you meet is headed for an eternity without God?

By David Shibley

The stabbing words of a foreign exchange student studying in the United States still ring in my ear today: "I thought Christianity was important in this country," she said. "But now I know it isn't. I've been here for a year, and no one has talked to me about Jesus."

Christianity, by its very nature, is evangelistic. Christian missions is based on the assumption that people who are without Jesus Christ are lost. We are on a rescue mission with eternal consequences.

Our emotional involvement in missions will be in direct proportion to the strength of our belief in the doctrine of the lostness of mankind. The reason for much of our lethargy today lies at this point. Though we may give mental assent to this truth, often we do not emotionally come to grips with its consequences.

If people are lost outside of Christ, and if faith in Jesus Christ is the only avenue of redemption, what could possibly be a higher priority than spreading the gospel as far as we can, as fast as we can? Anything the church does that is not directly tied to evangelism is not unlike rearranging the furniture while the house is on fire.

As pastor Ted Haggard of New Life Church in Colorado Springs, Colorado, says, the first priority of churches in any city should be "making it hard to go to hell from that city."

In my opinion, no theological issue could be more crucial for evangelism and missions than how deeply we really believe that people without Christ are eternally lost, and that there is salvation in no one else but Jesus (SEE ACTS 4:12). This is the watershed theological issue for evangelicals as we enter the 21st century.

Hell Is Real

Today, even in theologically conservative circles, we are battling universalism—the belief that all people will eventually be saved. Some otherwise Bible-believing Christians question the reality of judgment, especially for those who have never heard the gospel.

It is not that they have formally removed their belief in hell. There is simply an eerie silence as many endeavor to sort out what they hold to be true.

Universalism is an ancient heresy. It began in the Garden of Eden when the serpent told Adam and Eve, "You will not surely die" (GEN. 3:4, NKJV). One of its first proponents was Origen of Alexandria, and it was later condemned by the church.

Different shades of the teaching have periodically appeared, most noticeably in post-Reformation times in reaction to a strict doctrine of election, and in the 19th century when it was sometimes referred to as "the larger hope."

But Scripture leaves no doubt as to the final destiny of those without Christ. The Bible clearly describes a coming apocalypse: "When the Lord Jesus is revealed from heaven with His mighty angels, in flaming fire taking vengeance on those who do not know God, and on those who do not obey the gospel of our Lord Jesus Christ. These shall be punished with everlasting destruction from the presence of the Lord and from the glory of His power" (2 THESS. 1:7-9).

The most often quoted verse in the Bible clearly presents humanity's only two options: perishing or everlasting life. "For God so loved the world that He gave His only begotten Son, that whoever believes in Him should not perish but have everlasting life" (JOHN 3:16).

The subsequent verses remind us that God's disposition toward humankind is love and forgiveness: "For God did not send His Son into the world to condemn the world, but that the world through Him might be saved. He who believes in Him is not condemned; but he who does not believe is condemned already, because he has not believed in the name of the only begotten Son of God" (JOHN 3:17-18).

As Paul thought of his own people being lost, he wrote, "I have great sorrow and continual grief in my heart" (ROM. 9:2).

He added that he would be willing to give up his place in Christ and be separated from Him if by such a sacrifice others would be saved. Paul believed all people outside of Christ were lost, and it left him with a broken heart.

It is precisely this scandal of an unbroken heart that impedes evangelism today. The harvest is immense and ready to be gathered by those who have sown in tears. "Those who sow in tears shall reap in joy. He who continually goes forth weeping, bearing seed for sowing, shall doubtless come again with rejoicing, bringing his sheaves with him" (PS. 126:5-6).

The crown of rejoicing awaits those who win souls (SEE 1 THESS. 2:19-20). "Those who are wise shall shine like the brightness of the firmament, and those who turn many to righteousness like the stars forever and ever" (DAN. 12:3).

Jesus Christ declared that "no one comes to the Father except through Me" (JOHN 14:6). He spoke often of a terrible place of torment for those who were not reconciled to God. He told the story of an arrogant, wealthy man who, in hell, screamed and pleaded for just a drop of water.

The man cried, "I am tormented in this flame" (LUKE 16:24). Jesus said there would be those who would go "into the everlasting fire" (MATT. 25:41) and "into everlasting punishment" (MATT. 25:46).

The late W.T. Conner, president of Southwestern Baptist Seminary, once heard two students outside his office flippantly joking about hell. He met the young preachers in the hall, put his arms around their shoulders, and escorted them to a large picture window overlooking the city of Fort Worth, Texas.

As they gazed out the window, the younger men noticed that tears were coursing down Conner's cheeks. "Don't joke about hell, boys," he said softly. "People are going there. People are going there."

The destiny of those outside of Christ is no laughing matter. God is not desirous that anyone perish (SEE 2 PET. 3:9). We should share the heart of God.

Jesus tasted death for every person (SEE HEB. 2:9). That means the potential of redemption stretches to the entire human race. Christ was separated from the Father so that we might never need to be separated. Jesus, being infinite, suffered in a finite period of time what we, being finite, would have suffered in an infinite period of time.

What If People Never Hear?

A young person came to me some time ago with a troubled look on his face. "I believe the Bible," he told me. "But I just can't believe God would condemn someone who has never heard the gospel." This raises a difficult question: What happens to those who have never heard the truth?

In Romans chapter one, Paul makes an excellent case for the lostness of humanity. He reminds us that men and women are not only going to be lost when they die—they are born in sin as descendants of Adam and inherently separated from God.

The Bible says the unbelieving person is "condemned already" and that "the wrath of God abides on him" (JOHN 3:18, 36). Paul gives an airtight argument that every person stands accountable to God because of the light of conscience and the testimony of God in creation.

This testimony of nature is sometimes called "general revelation." Creation's general revelation of God powerfully preaches a person's accountability to his or her Creator. However, only the specific revelation of God in Jesus Christ shows how we can be justified before this holy Creator.

According to Paul, even the remotest of peoples are "without excuse" because of the light of conscience and nature. Yet only the light of the world, Jesus Christ, can bring them salvation.

It is important to understand that rejection of the gospel is not the only criterion for lostness. Humanity is already lost because of sin. "For all have sinned and fall short of the glory of God" (ROM. 3:23). We are sinners because of the wrongs we have done. But we are also sinners because of who we are—children of Adam.

God has gone to the very limits of boundless love to prevent humankind from perishing: God incarnate became sin incarnate on the cross. It is too much to fathom fully. Yet it is wonderfully true.

As we moved toward judgment, God intervened personally through Christ. "He is the atoning sacrifice for our sins, and not only for ours but also for the sins of the whole world" (1 JOHN 2:2).

The question of the lostness of those who have not heard the gospel is a vital issue. It must be resolved in one's heart before missionary passion can flow in fullness.

While the question is usually raised in sincerity, the one who doubts the lostness of those who haven't heard should carry that argument to its logical conclusion: If those who haven't heard are not accountable, then we should immediately rush to every missionary home and prevent every national worker from reaching any further.

After all, what if those previously unaccountable were to hear the gospel and reject it? They would then be accountable. The missionary would have done them a terrible disservice.

Such a line of reasoning would have to conclude that the kindest thing we could do for unreached humanity would be to stop preaching the gospel. Such reasoning dwarfs missionary advance.

But the truth is that those who have not heard the gospel are just as lost as those who have heard and rejected it. Therefore, the most benevolent, humanitarian activity in the world is preaching the gospel.

When the gospel message is received, the benefits begin immediately. Time and again, social transformation has resulted from the infiltration of the gospel into a society. But the benefits are also eternal. Those who hear and obey the gospel now possess eternal life. Dick Hillis, founder of Overseas Crusades, brings the issue to a verdict:

"If those who have not heard will somehow be saved, would it not then be best if they did not hear? Did Christ misguide His followers when He sent Paul throughout all Asia Minor and Europe? Or when He sent William Carey to India, Hudson Taylor to China and tens of thousands of missionaries around the world?

"If the unevangelized are not lost, is not the mission program

of the church a ludicrous blunder? Are millions of dollars
spent on a useless program? If the unreached are not lost,
does not the Scripture become a bundle of contradictions,
the Savior become a false teacher, the Christian message
become 'much ado about nothing?'"

All evidence points in the other direction. Most of the adherents
of the world's great religions are sincere. Yet sincerity is not what
saves us. Only faith in the finished work of Jesus Christ brings
salvation.

Holy Scripture does not suggest any alternative plan. We have
a distinct message—the only message that can set humanity's
captives free. The Christian message does not parrot other religions. Our faith is gloriously unique.

The Rescue Operation

In light of Jesus' sacrifice, we must go to the lost—endued with
the Spirit's power to actualize that for which Christ died. It was this
motivation that spurred Nikolaus von Zinzendorf and the Moravian
missionaries "to win for the Lamb the reward of His sacrifice." The
apostle Paul cried, "Necessity is laid upon me; yes, woe is me if I
do not preach the gospel!" (1 Cor. 9:16).

John Knox pleaded on his knees, "Give me Scotland, or I die."
Hudson Taylor, as a young man in England, cried to God, "I feel
that I cannot go on living unless I do something for China." Robert
Arthington could not go overseas but, through sacrifice, helped
send others. He lived in a single room, cooked his own meals
and gave more than $500,000 to missions. At the end of his life
he wrote, "Gladly would I again make the floor my bed, a box my
chair, another box my table, rather than that men should perish for
want of the knowledge of the Savior."

Each of these men had a heart pumping with what Oswald J.
Smith called "a passion for souls." Do you have that passion? Do
you long for more? The believer who is intimate with the Holy Spirit
is advantaged here. Why? "Because the love of God has been
poured out in our hearts by the Holy Spirit" (Rom. 5:5).

Late one night a concerned lighthouse keeper watched as a violent
storm erupted at sea. Suddenly the seasoned keeper saw the faint

SOS of a ship in distress. Instinctively he turned to his young apprentice and commanded, "Let's go!"

Horrified, the apprentice retorted, "But, sire, if we go out there, we may never come back."

The old keeper of the lighthouse paused and put his hand on the young man's shoulder. "Son," he responded, "we have to go out. We don't have to come back."

No one doubts that there is great peril in penetrating the final frontiers. But that is not the issue. What matters is that people are perishing.

We have to go to them. Are you willing to be on the rescue team?

Bio
David Shibley is a missionary strategist, author and president of Global Advance in Dallas. He spends most of his time training indigenous pastors to serve mission fields in developing nations.

10

Just Open Your Mouth And Share Jesus!

By Jerry Wiles

Jesus' top priority when He came into the world was to seek and save the lost. He now lives in you and me to carry out that same purpose. But even though most Christians would agree that sharing the gospel is something they should do, and want to do, evangelism remains a weak link in our lives.

Evangelism should be our strong suit. The more we identify with Jesus and commit to His plan and purpose, the more sensitive we become to our mission-carrying out the Great Commission.

The apostle Paul tells us in 2 Corinthians 5:17 that when we are in Christ, we are a new creation. The result of being a new creation is that we are ministers of reconciliation. This is not something you have to go to seminary for. It is part of the package deal-part of your salvation.

We are ambassadors for Christ. This means that we, as children of God, are representatives of Jesus. We are to reflect the likeness of our heavenly Father and honor and glorify Him. Having a conscious aware-ness of that truth is a great motivation to share Christ with others.

So how do we break out of our negative stereotypes and attitudes toward witnessing?

The key is to change the way we think about evangelism. Rather than approaching it as a duty, we should view it as serving people and sharing life in Christ. Just think of yourself as a good news reporter.

The way you see yourself is vitally important to the way you relate to others. If you see yourself the way God sees you-as a new creation, complete in Christ and an able minister of the new covenant-you will be more alert to the needs of others and more responsive to the Holy Spirit's work of redemption. When we, as followers of Jesus, come to grips with who He is in us and who we are in Him, we will be more intentional about sharing Him with others.

I came to this awareness more than 25 years ago, and it changed my life. I began to share Christ and see others come to Him on a regular basis. The realization that Christ was alive and living in me was a tremendous incentive to reach out to others and share with them how He could give them abundant and eternal life as well.

When we yield ourselves to the Lord, we have the privilege of being His instruments of righteousness in redeeming His creation (SEE ROM. 6:13). The Holy Spirit is at work all the time, everywhere, drawing people to Christ. And exciting things happen when we take advantage of the opportunities He puts in front of us.

Recognizing Opportunity

Driving through Kansas several years ago, I spotted a workman up ahead flagging traffic because of road construction. My car was the first in a long line of cars stopped, and the flagman was standing next to my window. He told me there would be a five-minute delay.

I had been driving for several hours and had been meditating on John 6:63, where Jesus said, "The words that I speak to you are spirit, and they are life" (NKJV). The Lord impressed me that because Christ was in me, the words I spoke could produce life in others.

I knew God wanted me to share the gospel with the flagman. But my first thought was that five minutes wasn't enough time. Then the Lord asked, "How much time does it take?" I got the message.

So I asked the man, "Have you seen any signs of spiritual awakening around here?" He wasn't sure what I meant by that, so I explained: "Have you noticed how more people have come to an awareness of their need for the Lord in recent days?"

Without hesitation, he answered, "I don't know about anybody else, but I know I need the Lord."

At that point I simply asked if he was aware that Jesus Christ, God's Son, died on the cross for his sins and that He rose from the dead so he could be forgiven and receive eternal life. The man said he was aware of that. I asked if he had ever experienced the new birth, and he said no. When I asked if he would like to experience it, he said yes.

I shared briefly from Romans 10 about repentance and faith and the fact that he didn't have to be in a church building or go through a long religious ritual to be saved. I told him the Lord was right there with us, and we could include Him in our conversation.

I said that we didn't even have to bow our heads and close our eyes. We could just talk to God, and he could invite Jesus into his life. The man prayed, and I gave him some gospel literature.

As soon as we were done, the flagman at the other end of the construction work gave a signal, and I was on my way. The encounter had taken less than five minutes. The Lord can work in brief time slots-we just need to be ready.

Every situation is unique because people are unique. But the Holy Spirit is creative in the way He prepares peoples' hearts and in how He works through each of us to share the good news.

Remember that it is God's work through us-not our work for Him-that produces lasting fruit. We do not have to persuade or convince people to receive Christ. That is the work of the Holy Spirit.

When it comes to winning others to Christ, it is important that our lives reflect His character. However, a Christlike lifestyle alone is not enough if we fail to tell others about Him. We must be intentional about sharing His life and the message of salvation with others.

Keep in mind that you don't have to have any particular spiritual gift or specialized training to bring others to Christ. He lives in you, so you already have everything you need. The Holy Spirit will guide and teach you as you reach out with the love of Jesus. Although education and training are important and helpful, you can start where you are with what you have.

Some time ago in a shopping mall, I engaged a Hindu busi-nessman in conversation about spiritual matters. I gave him a booklet titled How to Know God.

He told me that he had been in the United States for 15 years, and no one had ever explained to him how he could know God personally.

I was deeply touched as the man said that he had prayed twice a day, every day, since he was a little boy to get to know God, but he had always thought it was too hard. I shared the gospel with him, we prayed together, and he invited Christ into his life.

The flagman on the road and the Hindu businessman both had something in common: prepared hearts. In fact, there are probably more lost people prepared to receive Christ today than there are Christians actively inviting them to respond to the love of Christ.

The most effective ministry encounters are usually with long-term relationships: our families, co-workers and those we interact with regularly. However, think of all those short-term encounters we have with hotel maids, restaurant servers, janitors, security guards and store clerks. There are opportunities everywhere if we are alert and sensitive to the Holy Spirit.

I have found that if I pray each morning and ask the Lord to set up encounters with people who have prepared hearts, He faithfully answers my prayers and gives me the words to share.

You will have great confidence in sharing Christ if you are aware of God's presence with you and the fact that His Word doesn't return to Him void but accomplishes the purpose for which He sent it. Remember that "the Word of God is living and powerful, and sharper than any two-edged sword" (HEB. 4:12).

The apostle Paul said, "For I am not ashamed of the gospel of Christ, for it is the power of God to salvation for everyone who believes" (ROM. 1:16). When you share God's Word, the Holy Spirit will bear witness to the truth and convict others of their need for God.

Making Yourself Available

Not everyone you share Christ with will be receptive. In fact, most may not be ready to respond at that time. Often you will sow the seed of God's Word in a person's heart, and someone else will reap at a later date. What matters is your availability to be used by God.

I once approached a shoeshine man in a hotel lobby. I greeted him and just asked this question: "Has anyone talked with you about the Lord and how you can have a personal relationship with Him?" The man reached under his chair and pulled out a gospel booklet.

"Yeah, someone gave this to me this morning," he said. I was able to affirm the presentation of the gospel, which someone else had already given, and lead him in prayer to receive Christ.

First Corinthians 3:7 teaches that some plant, some water and others reap the harvest. God gives the increase. We are His co-laborers. It is exciting to know that when we step out in faith, we have a new opportunity to make Him known.

With God's anointing, even the little things we say or do can be used by Him to touch people's lives and change their eternal destinies. Making eye contact, smiling, waving or offering a friendly greeting can open the door for connecting with people and often to share Christ.

I remember giving an enthusiastic greeting to a shuttle bus driver as I met him at a revolving door in a hotel. He turned to me and said, "Haven't we met before?"

I said, "I don't think so, but we may have a mutual friend."

He asked who that might be, and I said: "The Lord Jesus Christ. Do you know Him?" It turned out that he knew about Him, but he had never trusted Christ personally as His Lord and Savior. After sharing further with him, I invited him to pray with me and ask Christ into his life-and he did.

You don't have to share Christ and seek to bring others to Him in the same way I do or as anyone else does. Each of us is unique and equipped in different ways to reveal Christ's life and demon-strate His love and grace to those around us.

A pastor I know used to say, "God is not as interested in your ability as He is in your availability; and He is not as interested in your scholarship as He is in your relationship." If we simply respond to the light God gives us, and if we love, trust and obey Him, then He will use us in the lives of those He brings across our paths.

Jesus said in Mark 1:17, "Follow Me, and I will make you become fishers of men." If you and I focus on following Him-that is, living in union with Him-He will make us to become His witnesses, His harvesters.

Recently I shared the gospel and prayed with a woman I had just met. She asked me, "Why didn't someone tell me this sooner?"

Think of all the people who you cross paths with who may simply be waiting for someone to tell them the good news.

So many Christians today are sincere in their commitment and effort, but they are striving in the energy of their own human resources. Many are trying hard, but are seeing little fruit. I can certainly identify with them.

In the early part of my walk with God, I had a desire and made an effort to be like Jesus. Then I learned that I didn't have what it takes to be like Him. Along with that I made the wonderful discovery that there is only one person who can be like Jesus Christ-and that is Jesus Christ Himself.

The exciting news is that Jesus is prepared to communicate His life through you to those around you. What a joy and adventure to just be along for the ride-to be in Christ and let Him live His life in and through us.

Someone has said that the real Christian life is just Jesus Christ. It is the life He lived then and lives now, through Himself, in us. We have the great joy of sharing with others what He has so graciously shared with us.

The greatest of all human experiences is coming into a spiritual and eternal relationship with the Creator of the universe through His only Son.

The second greatest experience in this life is being instrumental in others coming into that relationship, which translates them out of the kingdom of darkness and into the kingdom of His dear Son.

Just think-not only do we have a home in heaven for all eternity, but we also get to take others with us. We can be a part of increasing the population of heaven. Think of all those you will see in heaven who will thank you for something you said or did that influenced them to make a decision that changed their destiny from eternity without Jesus to a life filled forever with Him.

Bio
Jerry Wiles is assistant vice president for church relations at Houston Baptist University and author of How to Win Others to Christ (Thomas Nelson). He and his wife, Sheila, live in Sugar Land, Texas.

How Not to Share Your Faith

Many Christians are intimidated by the thought of evangelism. But talking about your faith is nothing to be afraid of. You may be the only person who shares Jesus with your friend. Don't blow the opportunity.

1. **Don't ask people, "Are you a Christian?"** Some believe they are Christians because they were baptized as babies or simply because they are Americans.

2. **Don't ask, "Are you born again?"** Not everyone knows what that means without an explanation. It sounds weird to those who don't attend church.

3. **Don't judge.** Don't assume that others don't know Christ just because they don't use the same terminology you do. Some people are followers of Christ, but "saved" or "born again" is not a part of their vocabulary.

4. **Don't use Christian jargon.** Terms like "saved," "sanctified" or "washed in the blood" can be a real turnoff. Explain the salvation message in simple, relevant, everyday terms to clearly communicate biblical truth.

5. **Don't rush things.** Don't assume that a person is converted to Christ as a result of your praying with them. Don't announce, "Now you are saved!" Always follow up to answer questions and confirm their commitment.

6. **Don't interfere with a person's work responsibility.** For example, a busy mealtime in a restaurant is not the right time to engage a server in a lengthy conversation. He or she could be fired because of your insensitivity.

7. **Don't argue.** Focus on Christ and the cross and everyone's need for Him. Don't get sidetracked by unimportant theological or political issues that divide people.

8. **Don't close the door on those who may reject the gospel.** The seeds you sow now may produce fruit later. Keep channels of communication open. Be lovingly persistent and trust God with the outcome.

Top 10 Ways to Start a Conversation About God

Do you find it difficult to start a conversation when you feel the nudge to share your faith? Witnessing doesn't have to sound forced or fake. These simple ice-breakers can lead to sincere discussions that may lead someone to Christ:

1. After a greeting or casual conversation, you can ask, "Have you noticed how many people today are thinking more about their need for God?" Their answer will help you perceive where they are spiritually.

2. Ask people you meet if they have noticed any signs of spiritual awakening in their cities. This is another general, nonthreatening question.

3. Greet people with this question: "Has the Lord been good to you today?" Just bringing the Lord into your conversation will often open up a ministry opportunity.

4. At a Christian convention, concert or other gathering, you can ask security guards, janitorial staff or support personnel, "Has anyone talked with you about the Lord today?" You might follow up with, "Has anyone shared with you how you can know God personally?"

5. Give someone a Gospel of John or other portion of Scripture and say, "Here's a booklet that was written by a man who knew Jesus personally. It tells how you can know Him personally as well."

6. If you are talking to a religious person who may not really know Christ, ask him or her, "Have you had a desire for a more personal, intimate relationship with God?"

7. Talking to family members or close friends about God can be awkward. A good approach is to ask, "Is something going on in your life that I can pray with you about?" This will often lead to further discussion.

8. A good way to introduce a spiritual dimension into a conversation is to say: "You might be interested to know that a growing number of people are coming to an awareness of the need for something or someone outside of themselves. Have you noticed that?"

9. Share your testimony. Begin by saying, "Would you mind if I share with you how I came to have real peace and joy in my life and an assurance that I'll go to heaven when I die?"

10. If someone seems receptive to spiritual things, ask him or her, "Would you like to know for sure that your sins are forgiven?"

11

Out Where the Sinners Are

By Chris Maxwell

Recently while browsing through a Barnes & Noble bookstore with a friend, I struck up a conversation with the store manager. He seemed friendly and eager to know more about us, so halfway through our conversation I told him we were both pastors.

He was shocked—not because he doesn't like ministers, but because he'd never really had a decent conversation with a Christian.

"I normally only hear from Christians when they are mad," he told me.

The three of us sat down at the coffee bar. The manager told tales about religious people who had called, written or walked in his store to inform him they would never do business with him because of objectionable books or Halloween displays.

The man thanked us for being different and then excused himself so he could get back to work. My thoughts were racing so fast I found it hard to finish my bagel. No best seller could have taught us what we learned from this honest man.

I asked myself, How can believers shine a light and promote the gospel in a sinful, wicked world? Maybe, just maybe, God wants people today to follow the example of Jesus. Time and technology have changed, but yesterday's techniques can still touch today's world.

Sitting idly as silent witnesses is not enough. Lumbering ahead to peddle words without the Spirit is too much. We need to reach the lost as Jesus did. He models a personal, realistic approach to speaking forth the good news.

Let's review a biblical story to discover the steps Jesus used to initiate conversation with the people He met and open the door for true evangelism.

1. Jesus broke the rules.

Alone and worn from His journey, Jesus sat by a well. His robe flashed no religious logo.

Then a woman approached to draw water.

The middle of the day was a strange time for her to undertake this task. People habitually took care of such business before the sun became their enemy. Gathering in the morning or evening hours made the climate work in their favor, as labor turned into an arena for conversation. They socialized as they worked.

Not this woman. She came during the heat of the day, revealing her standing with society. Enduring the relentless afternoon sun was better than suffering the silence of a condemning group gathered around a well.

Jesus was not put off by her presence. In fact, His choosing not to leave when the woman drew near underscored the first dynamic of evangelism illustrated by this story: Jesus broke the rules.

Devout Jews despised the people of Samaria, but not Jesus. He refused to allow man's religious rules to hinder His purpose.

Travel through a sinful city? Converse with a Samaritan who was not only a woman but also a person of ill-repute? Unheard of.

Not for Jesus. He came to do the will of His Father without concern for religious or social tradition. Children, sinners, prostitutes, thieves, poor and uneducated people—He touched all those ignored by religious rule-keepers.

The clean hands of strict legalists would not dare applaud His efforts. But He continued. And He reminded listeners of His purpose: "Those who are well have no need of a physician, but those who are sick. I have not come to call the righteous, but sinners, to repentance" (Luke 5:31-32, NKJV).

Jesus remained on course despite strong winds of pharisaical opposition that sought to blow Him in another direction. He broke rules; they judged Him guilty by association. Their muttering confirmed that He remained true to His agenda: "This Man receives sinners and eats with them" (Luke 15:2).

Eating with people during Christ's day carried social significance.

Christ embraced people others avoided. He associated with the guilty to reach them, not to become like them. But in order to reach them, He first entered their world.

Let's not become more comfortable criticizing sinners than converting them. The color of a person's skin or the habits of a person's life must never prohibit us from reaching out to them. It is imperative that we welcome all.

Jesus allowed the woman to approach. Then He initiated conversation.

2. Jesus broke the ice.

We often wonder how to begin a discussion with an unbeliever or how to channel dialogue toward the gospel. It is awkward making the transition from career questions or weather expectations to spiritual realities. But the Holy Spirit possesses an amazing ability to steer conversations toward eternal matters if we flow with Him.

We say we believe that people without Christ lack what can help them the most. Yet many times we speak as salesmen not sold on our own product. Jesus talked, listened and observed. He found common ground.

Thirsty beside a well, He asked the woman for water. She had the power to give it. What a wonderful way to break the ice, guiding discussion in a good direction. The right words at the right time can open doors of great opportunity.

Jesus did not use the same phrases every time He reached out to someone. He observed a situation and spoke words that moved toward truth. Now that task is our role, our calling.

Often, as we seek to reach out, our behavior will break the ice more than our conversation. Actions of love do speak louder than words.

Years ago a storm hit hard in southern Mexico. The dangerous weather washed out a bridge necessary for travel between two key cities. Hoping to quickly solve their problem, a large group gathered for a night of hurried repair.

Missionary Larry Myers had labored among these people but had struggled to build a good rapport with them. Though he had previously planted churches in hundreds of Mexican communities, at this place he found spiritual resistance.

He prayed, hoped and wondered how to reach the people. Then he saw that their problem provided an opportunity to break the ice.

As the men toiled, Myers purchased a truckload of tacos and drove to the work site. When he arrived, he provided food and assisted their labor. His act of kindness broke the ice in a town that now serves as a key location for his national outreach. As a result of his involvement, the city shifted in a positive spiritual direction.

3. Jesus broke the news.

What purpose would we serve by gaining friends and never telling them about Jesus? Lifestyle witnessing opens the door to evangelism, but eventually we must verbalize the story.

Jesus perceived that the Samaritan woman was thirsty for more than a drink of water. Her shifts from man to man indicated a craving for acceptance that eluded surface relationships. Jesus did not preach—He probed.

Listening ears and warm hearts are wonderful. But we must not conclude with only hearing and caring. We must tell people about eternal hope. Jesus moved toward ultimate truth, informing the woman that He was the Messiah.

I learned during my teen-age years how important it is to bring the good news to others; an experience I had with a friend of mine convinced me I needed to be more aggressive in sharing my faith.

We were both point guards on our high school basketball team and were two years apart in age. My friend led the team; I hoped to take his place my junior year after he graduated.

Before he left school, my friend heard the gospel. He shared his experience with me, concluding his testimony with a smile. But as I walked off with him, the expression on his face changed to real concern. He asked me to become a Christian.

When I told him I had been one for a few years, he stopped walking. Staring at me, he asked, "If you have been a Christian all this time, why did you never tell me I needed to become one?"

His question pricked me. If I truly believed what I thought I believed, why had I talked with him about everything—sports, music, school, family—except what mattered most?

My whole attitude changed. I began to witness to classmates, teammates and strangers. I spoke about the gospel, taught about it, wrote about it. God reminded me that we live on a planet covered with thirsty people.

Jesus knew the woman at the well needed more than a drink. She came there to draw water, yet she was thirsty for so much more. And she found something greater than what could come out of a well.

In the Messiah she found love. She found One who knew her more fully than anyone could know her, than she could know herself. After thirsting a long time, she finally found what she was looking for in Christ.

How many of our friends are thirsty for the Living Water the woman at the well encountered? What will we do to make sure they take a drink?

No, we should not become like the world. But neither should we hide from those Jesus died to save. Not if we care. Not if we long to fulfill His call.

So many more wait by the well. Let us pour out the drink of glory to give them life—today.

Bio
Chris Maxwell is the pastor of Evangel Assembly of God in Orlando, Florida. He likes to hang out with sinners at bookstores, ball games and on the Internet.

20 Ways to Reach the Lost

How can you demonstrate God's love in your community?

Here are just a few things Jesus might do:

▶▶ **Pray fervently.** If your church has an intercessory prayer group, participate in it. If not, start one, and encourage others to join you in interceding regularly for the lost in your city.

▶▶ **Be an active school parent.** Prayer may not be allowed in the classroom, but the government can't stop your light from shining in a school environment. Become friends with the principal, teachers and other parents.

▶▶ **Celebrate holidays in style.** Gather neighbors, co-workers or relatives for Christmas or Easter. Then tell the old, old story of Jesus' birth or resurrection in a brand-new way.

▶▶ **Join a club.** Writers' groups, music clubs and other common-interest organizations can open doors for you to share the gospel. Don't avoid non-Christian gatherings.

▶▶ **Coach a Little League team.** Coaching or playing sports can initiate friendships and help you reach the younger generation.

▶▶ **Build a cross-cultural bridge.** Become friends with someone who looks different and has a different history.

▶▶ **Adopt a child.** We Christians admit that unwanted children need a home, but are we willing to play the role of parent to them?

▶▶ **Become a pen pal.** Prisoners have time to read mail. Who's going to write them?

▶▶ **Get a workout partner.** Your lost neighbor needs exercise, too. Ask him or her to join you for regular visits to the fitness center.

▶▶ **Who says you can't visit a bar?** Jesus didn't let religious people dictate where He could or couldn't go; neither should you.

▶▶ **Bless your food server.** Restaurant workers often complain that church people are more rude and tip less generously than others. Let's change our image! Be friendly, listen and don't just leave a gospel tract; leave a big tip.

▸▸ Feed the homeless. Local ministries in your area are touching these lonely people. Get involved.

▸▸ Share a meal and a movie. Invite an adult neighbor over for a home-cooked dinner or a backyard barbecue, then watch a wholesome video.

▸▸ Send a card. Surprise unbelievers in your office with an expression of kindness on birthdays, holidays or the anniversary of a painful memory.

▸▸ Help someone in crisis. Volunteer at a local hospital or with a meals-on-wheels program.

▸▸ Start an office Bible study. Get permission first, then have an informal time of sharing over a brown-bag lunch.

▸▸ Comfort someone dying of AIDS. Many cities need hospice volunteers to minister to the terminally ill.

▸▸ Become a Big Brother or Sister. Scores of young children are raised in single-parent homes and need the influence of another adult to help them grow to maturity. Make one part of your life.

▸▸ Reach out to children in your neighborhood. Invite neighborhood children into your home (with their parents' permission, of course) for cookies, a story or a swim in your pool, and share the love of Jesus with them.

▸▸ Be a friend. Nowhere in the Bible are we told to shun contact with unbelievers. We are called to love and serve the people we meet in school, at work and in our communities. Listen, offer encouragement and wait for opportunities to share Christ.

12

You Need To Live Upside Down

Most of us spend our lives striving to possess things,
power and position. But true success in God's kingdom
requires us to do the opposite.

By Tommy Barnett

I stood in the sanctuary of the empty Angelus Temple, the famous church built by Foursquare founder Aimee Semple McPherson, and found myself close to tears. I looked up at the slate-blue dome directly overhead. It was well lit and resplendent, though the rest of the sanctuary was dim. The mural of a resurrected Jesus behind the platform still inspired awe, and the stained-glass windows two stories high gave the feel of a modern cathedral.

But this was no ordinary cathedral. For years, the innovative Sister Aimee had used this as her pulpit to the world. In the 1930s she was more famous than any film or music star. Thousands flocked every Sunday to hear her preach and to see her many spectacles, illustrated sermons, great choirs and dramatic presentations.

Most of all they came because she loved them. She wasn't just putting on a show. She was feeding the hungry—one and a half million of them during the Great Depression.

She was giving people hope during hard times. She was delivering the gospel to a city desperate for a true message among the glitter of movies.

Sister Aimee had learned the secret to success in the spiritual kingdom: giving oneself away. According to the Bible, we will succeed in direct proportion to how much we give ourselves away—not just in ministry, but in marriage, in raising children, in friendships, in business and even in recreation.

I know it doesn't make sense. By nature we would rather possess than share, have than give. But if you follow the Lord long enough, one day it clicks: Joy is not living palms up—it's living palms down. Nobody has become happy from what they possessed, but anyone can increase their happiness by giving.

Giving is truly the key to blessing. I have seen more souls saved in the last four years of my ministry than in the 47 years before. I have seen more money come through my hands for the ministry recently than ever before.

Why? Not just because I have better staff or a better strategy than ever but because we have learned to focus more and more on servanthood, on downward mobility, on giving everything away. We have found that the more we give away, the more God pours resources and surprise blessings into our hands.

Do you really believe it's better to give than to receive? Does the thought frighten you? In their minds, most Christians believe this principle works—but few actually practice it. Some see this tidbit of wisdom merely as a nice suggestion, never realizing the seismic power it holds.

I admit, it's not easy to convince yourself that the Bible and only the Bible is right. When it says, "It is more blessed to give than to receive" (Acts 20:35, NIV), we should accept that as 100 percent correct—but often we don't. When it says: "The greatest among you will be your servant. For whoever exalts himself will be humbled, and whoever humbles himself will be exalted" (MATT. 23:11-12), we should accept it as a rock-solid fact—and act on it. That's the stuff of revolutions.

But most people never reach that place in their lives.

Debunking the Myth of Lack

Why do we struggle with the principle of giving? A major hindering factor is the world in which we live—it encourages us to hold tightly to everything we have. Things always seem to be running out. Our cell phones have limited minutes and limited calling areas. Our cars can hold only so much gas. Our vacation time runs out. So does our patience, our energy, our attention. Our monthly budget seems to disappear down rabbit holes.

On a global scale we are told that the oil supply will run out in a few decades and that there isn't enough room on the planet for all the people who will be born. Some say the supply of fresh water is dwindling; others say the ozone layer is thinning too quickly.

We are conditioned to think in terms of limits, and therefore the world operates on the principle of lack. The world says you start from a position of not having anything, and you have to grab and claw your way to a place of having enough. In the world, the successful man is the one who stores up the most.

God approaches life from the opposite angle. He operates on the principle of plenty. In God's kingdom, the successful man or woman is the one who gives the most away.

The world says, "He who dies with the most toys wins." The kingdom says, "He who gives away the most wins."

God doesn't see the cup half full or half empty—He sees it over-flowing!

From God's perspective, words such as "scarce resources," "conserve," "save up" and "limited" are meaningless. His is a world without limits, and we can connect to it.

I'm reminded of the way the fuel tank of an Air Force fighter plane is refilled while the plane is in the air. A fuel-bearing tanker flies right above the plane and extends a gas pipeline down to the fighter plane's tank. The fighter plane doesn't have to land; it is refueled in mid-flight. That's what God does for us.

Our minds are juxtaposed between a world that says lack is the rule and a God who says we lack nothing. The challenge is to act based on God's truth. We can demonstrate our belief in it by giving away as much as we can.

Most Christians I know are sincere about wanting to please God, yet many of them are frustrated and end up striving for God's promises. There are plenty of books and teaching tapes about how to have more peace or joy or good relationships. In a way, that advice can encourage the kind of chasing after worldly things that God prohibits us from doing. Yes, we may be chasing the right things, but it may be done in the wrong spirit—a spirit of striving and worry.

Sad to say, I believe Christian books can take advantage of this by "selling" solutions—blessings, joy and peace—as if they can be chased down and grabbed. The advice tastes good, like ice cream on the tongue, and of course it's coated in Bible verses. But by the time it reaches our stomachs there's nothing there, and the striving makes us ill.

Such striving encourages us to believe that we lack something. It clouds the fact that we already possess the promises of God. In fact, God's promises don't need to be hunted down. He has given them to us already!

The secret, I believe, is realizing that in the kingdom life there is no such thing as want. In Christ, we have all we need right now. We don't need books or teachings to bring us closer to the promises.

Many believers think that in Christ potentially we have everything we need. They think we can access everything we need only if we pray hard enough, read the right books or learn the right spiritual formulas.

Such a belief arises from a lack mentality. In truth, whether we are poor or rich ("whether living in plenty or in want," as Paul talks about in Philippians 4:12), we have everything we need. That means everything—from spiritual things to material things. For that reason Paul could say, "I have learned to be content whatever the circumstances" (v. 11). He didn't chase down what he wanted. He knew he possessed it already in Christ.

Beloved, there is no need to search all over for the latest key to God's benefits. As a believer, even as you read these words you possess the promises. God can't make His Word any truer. It's up to you to flip the switch from unbelief to belief.

When we flip the switch we discover that we don't need to chase after the same things the rest of the world chases after—money or position, personal fulfillment or tranquility. To run after those things—or even after the things God wants us to have—is the first sign that we don't really have them. When we really believe we already have them, we can relax.

That, in turn, makes us better givers.

The Kingdom Way

Life works only when lived upside down—that's the kingdom way. It works only when lived backward from what you would naturally expect. Giving yourself away is not just a nice thought. Giving is actually better than receiving—whether we like it or not. God made His kingdom to work that way, and if we don't play by His rules, we won't get His results.

I have found that when I plan or preach or pray without a giving spirit, my investment comes back small. But when I go into it by giving all the energy and fervency I have, I find myself replenished, and the investment multiplies.

That's how the "kingdom engine" works. You are free to put in it whatever you want, but the only way to get it to run effectively is to fill it with giving.

This principle of giving yourself away is more powerful than any automobile engine. It's even more powerful than an energy plant or a booster rocket. It doesn't move just tons of steel—it moves mountains. It shapes destinies, sets the course of history, defines how governments and societies behave, inspires inventions. Literally, it is a force that no man can stop. Indeed, giving is one of the few things nobody can stop you from doing. Even if you were shackled and imprisoned, you could still give yourself away.

But you can give only what you have in your heart. If you have worry, you give worry. Maybe you're the kind of person who worries about money, and now you're breeding that worry in your children or spouse.

If you have anger, you give anger. Maybe you blow up when things don't go as planned. Proverbs 19:3 says, "A man's own folly ruins his life, yet his heart rages against the Lord." In other words, an angry person ruins his own life and then blames God for the results.

But when you truly have the peace of God, it spreads to others like a beautiful fragrance. I have found that the most tranquil, faith-filled, happy people are those who give of themselves at every opportunity. They have risen to that heavenly level where nothing stops them from giving.

This is the highest—but not the only level. There are actually three levels of living and giving.

One is the hellish level, where people return evil for good. When the Jewish leaders put Jesus to death and treated Him shamefully, they were acting on this hellish level. We see glimpses of this in our day when acts of kindness are paid back with evil.

Another is the human level, where people return good for good and evil for evil. Most people's idea of morality is, If you're nice to me, I'll be nice to you; but if you're mean to me, I'll be mean to you.

Third is the heavenly level, where people return good for evil. This is the level on which Jesus said we should live, though not many people live on it consistently. It means doing good to people who hurt you, steal from you or cheat you.

Living on this level doesn't really make sense—unless you see it from God's perspective. The Bible says that God is kind to the ungrateful and the wicked (see Is. 26:10).

Is that because He likes ingratitude and wickedness? No. It's because His character doesn't change no matter how men behave. He is the source of all goodness, and the only way to counteract evil is with goodness (see Rom. 12:21).

It is on the heavenly level that we realize God's supply of goodness has no end. We can afford to pour it out on friends and enemies alike without ever fearing that we'll run out. That's the level on which we're invited to live.

Sadly, the vast majority of people give to get. But Jesus tells us, "'Freely you have received, freely give'" (Matt. 10:8). I believe we ought to give because we already have received—and not just a small portion. Those who have God have everything.

Bio
Tommy Barnett is senior pastor of Phoenix (Arizona) First Assembly of God, one of America's largest churches. He is also a co-founder of the Los Angeles Dream Center, a ministry that reaches out to more than 30,000 people each week.

13

God Doesn't Bless Bigheads

Our culture worships celebrities and superheroes.
But in the kingdom of God, we are called to pursue humility.

By Larry Tomczak

I want to thank my Dad and Mom...," he began, smiling while trying to choke back the tears that were trickling down his face.

Ché Ahn, my "son in the faith," was standing before the congregation that Sunday morning more than 20 years ago, about to be ordained. While he was honoring his parents, I couldn't help feeling a little fatherly pride over the man I had spent years mentoring, and with whom I shared a wonderful friendship.

"I'm grateful to my family members...," he continued. Just the day before, I had officiated at his wedding.

"I also want to honor the men who have poured their lives into mine." He began listing the godly people—none nearly as close to him as I was—while throwing in remnants of stories and describing their unique contributions to his life.

Sitting on the front row, my thoughts began to drift. I wonder what he'll say when he gets to me? Sniffling a little and straightening my posture in my chair, I readied myself for the "big" moment when Ché would single me out as the spiritual father who had brought him to this hallowed place.

Ché concluded naming the various people, and the applause subsided. Then he stepped back from the microphone and said quietly, "There is one more man I want to honor today." His eyes scanned the hundreds present as I gathered my thoughts.

"I thank God for his role in the plan of God for my life." I cleared my throat, preparing to share a few words.

"Lastly, I...I...want to honor...Charles Schmitt [a wonderful Bible teacher whose teaching had influenced Ché]. Please stand." The crowd broke into applause as I sat there, stunned.

God had pulled a fast one on me!

As I concluded my clapping and made my way alongside the other leaders to lay hands on Ché in prayer, I did my best to conceal my sadness in being forgotten.

How could he overlook me? I thought. After all the years, all the time. No one had given to him as I had.

An hour later I drove home feeling physically spent and emotionally hurt. As the inevitable "Why?" circulated in my mind, I sensed the fingertip of God on my spirit. "I let this happen on purpose, My son," He said, "to reveal what was in your heart."

My good Shepherd was going bottom line, and He was right. I was exposed. God made me aware of my carnal desires for recognition and honor by allowing me to be overlooked.

Subduing my flesh, I eventually repented and let God know I was ashamed and truly sorry for my pride.

Today Ché remains my close friend as he leads the Harvest International Ministries (HIM) network of churches and serves as director for The Call, an international prayer movement. We both laugh now at the oversight, but I'm thankful for what happened. The lesson from God was loud and clear: He wants the people who serve Him to be men and women of humility.

God Doesn't Need Superheroes

The greatest danger lurking ahead of any pioneer is overconfidence. When you trust in your own abilities and seek recognition, you set yourself up for a fall. To be a pioneer of the spiritual sort, you must recognize how human you really are.

If you ever struggle with superhero tendencies, you are in good company. The apostle Paul struggled with pride, and as a result, God gave him a thorn in his flesh (see 2 Cor. 12:7-9).

The power for you to minister as a pioneer comes not from honed skills or extensive Bible knowledge (though both are important).

The power comes from your acknowledgement of your inabilities and God's abilities. God's power is made perfect in weakness, and His grace is released in your life when you deflect all honor from you to Him.

Throughout Scripture God makes it clear that He will not share His glory with another (SEE Is. 42:8; Ps. 115:1). When you withhold the glory that is due God, you will find Him opposing you.

The apostle Peter wrote: "All of you, clothe yourselves with humility toward one another, because, 'God opposes the proud but gives grace to the humble.' Humble yourselves, therefore, under God's mighty hand, that he may lift you up in due time" (1 PET. 5:5–6, NIV).

God isn't neutral or passive about proud people. He opposes them. The Greek word for "oppose" in this passage, antitasso, is a military term that literally means "to rage in battle against."

When you seek glory for yourself, when you take the credit for any success, you risk having God battle against you. And the one person you don't want resisting you is almighty God!

On the other hand, God gives grace to the humble. Pride places God against you; humility places God on your side and unleashes the powers of heaven on your behalf.

And notice, Peter doesn't write, "You are clothed with humility." He writes, "Clothe yourselves with humility." Humility is something God won't do for you. It's not a fruit of the Spirit that is a result of the Spirit's work.

Humility is an act of your will. That's why Peter writes further, "Humble yourselves, therefore, under God's mighty hand, that he may lift you up in due time" (1 PET. 5:6).

God isn't opposed to exalting you. In fact, He wants to—but He must be the One doing the exalting! Exalt yourself, and God will humble you. But humble yourself, and God will exalt you— according to His time line.

When you don't choose to be humble, it is easy to become uptight and believe that if you don't speak up for yourself, no one else will commend you. You may have the noblest reasons for drawing attention to yourself, but all of them are rooted in pride. Don't worry about being promoted. Be faithful in the little things, and God will make you a ruler over much (SEE MATT. 25:23).

When you promote yourself, you circumvent God's time line and process for promotion. Perhaps He wants to work on a few more character issues before moving you on—issues that will make the difference between being an effective leader and an ineffective leader.

Self-promotion is the pursuit of quantity over quality because it seeks quick results without having to prove itself first. It also places people in the position of trying to do God's work in the flesh, which requires much more effort than doing God's work by the power of the Spirit.

The Faceless Generation

As God revives and restores His church, He is building the ranks of His troops with men and women of character. In humility they will march forward, unconcerned about drawing attention to themselves or building their own kingdoms.

Prophetic leader Paul Cain refers to this mass of people as a "nameless, faceless generation." They are consumed solely with the glory of God and care not what accolades or awards are bestowed upon them.

Michael Brown often exhorts students and faculty at the FIRE School of Ministry by saying: "Don't forget why God brought us here. He is taking somebodies and turning them into nobodies for the glory of God!" The greatest aspiration you could ever have is to be a nobody for God.

"God works best with nothing," Mother Teresa once said. And that is God's nature—working best with nothing. Genesis 1:1 begins with these famous words, "In the beginning God created the heavens and the earth." God created the world out of nothing and then called it good (SEE GEN. 1:10).

When Jesus came to earth, He followed the same pattern. Read closely Paul's description of the incarnation of Jesus: "Do nothing out of selfish ambition or vain conceit, but in humility consider others better than yourselves...Your attitude should be the same as that of Christ Jesus: Who, being in very nature God, did not consider equality with God something to be grasped, but made himself nothing, taking the very nature of a servant, being made in human likeness. And being found in appearance as a man, he humbled himself and became obedient to death—even death on a cross!

"Therefore God exalted him to the highest place and gave him the name that is above every name, that at the name of Jesus every knee should bow, in heaven and on earth and under the earth, and every tongue confess that Jesus Christ is Lord, to the glory of God the Father" (PHIL. 2:3–11).

How does Paul describe Jesus' actions when He came to earth to save people from their sins?

▸▸ He made Himself nothing.

▸▸ He took the form of a servant.

▸▸ He humbled Himself.

▸▸ He became obedient to death on a cross.

And how did God the Father respond to Jesus' ultimate acts of humility?

▸▸ He exalted Jesus, giving Him the name that is above all names.

▸▸ He promised that all people will eventually bow their knees to Jesus and confess that Jesus is Lord.

▸▸ Most interesting of all is how Paul prefaces this weighty passage of Scripture: "Your attitude should be the same as that of Christ Jesus" (PHIL. 2:5).

Of course, you aren't God, and God will not someday have creation bow at your feet and declare that you are Lord. However, as you make yourself nothing, taking the form of a servant, humbling yourself and becoming obedient to death, God will exalt you. He will use you because you have become clay in the hands of the Master Potter.

Looking back over his 80 years of life, Billy Graham wrote in his magnificent autobiography, *Just As I Am*: "Most of all, if anything has been accomplished through my life, it has been solely God's doing, not mine, and He—not I—must get the credit." Billy Graham was a 20th century pioneer for the gospel who models what the heart of a 21st century pioneer should be like.

When the focus of your life is on yourself, you become fearful of man. You want to please people, and you seek their approval. But when the focus of your life is on God, you can venture wherever He calls you to go.

This is an area that God had to resolve in my life before releasing me into the next season of my ministry. For years I made little concessions and compromises to stay in the good graces of certain leaders and to avoid forfeiting privilege, promotion, provision or personal speaking opportunities.

By yielding to a fear of man I became enslaved to the pursuit of being recognized in ministry. My futile attempts to achieve approval and acceptance of certain people drove me even further away from the path God called me to follow.

This carnal, destructive pattern that had developed imperceptibly over many years had to be exposed and dismantled. What I needed was a deathblow to my sinful nature. So God brought me back to the place of being nothing, where I could choose to take on the form of a servant, humble myself and, most painfully, become obedient to death, nailing that self to the cross.

Finally, I could start over. But this time I was performing for an audience of one, God Himself. The result was a new dimension of freedom from bondage to man that I had never known before.

I enjoyed the new security that comes from pleasing the one who already loves and accepts me. I was free to set out again as a pioneer. I could say with Paul: "Am I now trying to win the approval of men, or of God? Or am I trying to please men? If I were still trying to please men, I would not be a servant of Christ" (GAL. 1:10).

Seemingly overnight, I jumped from overseeing a network of churches to planting a small church in the basement of my modest home. Straying from the "proven" methods of church planting I was accustomed with, I chose to establish a church birthed in the fires of revival.

But I must admit that my new beginning was quite humbling, even humiliating. While attending a men's conference in Florida I was approached by a leader of a large church with attendance in excess of 5,000. He began our conversation by asking, "So how large is your church in Atlanta?"

Ouch! Hearts are tested in moments like those! And what matters most to God is faithfulness before fruitfulness.

Get Your Heart Checked

Everyone should see a doctor at least once a year for a checkup. I think that same advice is good for Christians. At least once a year we should visit the Great Physician for a thorough examination of our spiritual condition.

Below are some penetrating questions that I hope you will ask yourself to help determine the state of your heart and your motivation for serving God.

1. Do I promote myself? Is it all about me and my ministry, or do I leave promotion to God while I go about the work He brings to me? (See Prov. 27:2; 25:6-7; Ps. 75:6).

2. Do I compete with others? Or am I secure in God wherever He places me, content to glorify only Him while He providentially works out His plan for my life? (See Jer. 45:5; Gal. 5:26; 1 Tim. 6:6).

3. Do I act out of a pure heart? Am I intent on pleasing God, or do my actions proceed from selfish ambition that only pleases me? (See James 3:16; Prov. 21:2; Phil. 2:3).

Periodically it is wise to ask yourself: Why am I doing what I'm doing? Who am I doing this for?

A dear friend of mine has a glowing résumé. At times in her life she has worked with political luminaries such as senators John Glenn and Barry Goldwater. At other times she has labored alongside Christian leaders such as Kenneth Copeland and Marilyn Hickey.

But currently she is following the call of God on her life by caring for her 84-year-old father. Yet Bessie is as aglow with the Spirit washing her father's feet as she is when she is in the limelight.

The reason? Her identity comes from her heavenly Father, not from how well she performs or from being recognized. She is simply serving in a different type of ministry during this season of her life. What would you do if you were in Bessie's shoes?

Don't be a somebody. Be a nobody through whom God builds His church and launches this generation into the final push that ushers in the return of Jesus Christ.

Bio
Larry Tomczak is the senior pastor of Christ the King Church in Atlanta. He is the author of six books, including Divine Appointments (Destiny Image).

Love
One Another

"And now abide faith,
hope, love, these three; but
the greatest of these is love."

1 Corinthians 13:13 NKJV

14

A Big Heart For the World

Florida pastor William Ilnisky rallied his small Florida church
to make a difference in the lives of African children who
were orphaned by the AIDS epidemic.

By Adrienne S. Gaines

Newsweek magazine doesn't normally bring Florida pastor William
Ilnisky to tears. But in February 1999 when he read a cover story
on the 10 million African children orphaned by AIDS, he suddenly
began to weep—and hardly stopped for two weeks.

"I found myself totally incapable of thinking about anything other
than that," Ilnisky says. "I spent most of that time crying and asking
God what to do about it."

Ilnisky believes his unusual reaction was God's way of speaking
to him, and the result was Sekelela (translated "rejoice") Africa's
Orphans, a ministry that provides health care, food and the gospel
to thousands of orphans in Zambia.

Back in 1999, he says he felt like "a teaspoon in an ocean," given
the enormity of the AIDS epidemic. Roughly 6,000 people were
dying daily in sub-Saharan Africa, with another 11,000 infected
each day. But as he shared his burden with his 150-member
congregation, Lighthouse Christian Center International in West
Palm Beach, a plan unfolded.

Longtime member and church staffer Delane Bailey, 36, dreamed
when she was a girl that she would some day set up clinics in
Africa. A native of Jamaica, she moved to the United States in
1983 to study biology. But as the years rolled by she "got involved
doing so many other things that were not Africa."

Trained as a missionary through the Vineyard School of Missions
in El Paso, Texas, Bailey had done midwifery and primary care in
Third World nations, including Mexico and the Philippines. She
helped build an orphanage in Uganda, and in Florida she assisted
people with HIV-AIDS and their families.

"I thought it would never happen," she says of her childhood dream. But as Ilnisky shared from the Newsweek article, Bailey says that "the vision came back alive to me, what we could do and some of the things we could implement. And right away I began working with the pastor to try to make contacts."

Once an Assemblies of God (AG) missionary, Ilnisky, 70, began corresponding with another AG missionary based in Zambia, and a year after Ilnisky first shared his burden, a small team made a trip to Zambia.

It was June 2000, and nearly 20 percent of the Zambian adult population was reportedly HIV-positive. The U.S. team had been told that many children no longer showed emotion because they had been so hardened by death. Ilnisky says children as young as 10 were heads of households, carrying younger siblings on their backs.

But Ilnisky says as the team began to lay hands on them that "all a sudden the loudest wailing and crying began to come out of these children. When the adults…heard the children crying, they were in absolute shock because these children did not cry. We watched in that moment as God began to do inner healing…and began to heal the wounds."

Bailey encouraged the children to pray for other orphans around the world. She showed them a globe that Ilnisky's wife, intercessory prayer leader Esther Ilnisky, had designed to teach children about the 10/40 Window, a region believed to be the least impacted by the gospel.

"Those kids began to weep," Bailey says. "First they wept for themselves, and then…they began to weep for the other children that were in similar situations."

"There's no way for us, even if we fill their stomachs, to heal their broken hearts," Ilnisky adds, "or to heal the scars of both Mother and Dad dying of AIDS, and them being ostracized because their parents have died of AIDS, and the village kicks them out, or their family throws them out to the street, and there's no one to care for them. That's true to thousands upon thousands of orphaned children in Zambia. And somehow God has to come on the scene and heal."

In addition to providing health care, Sekelela is developing manuals to train Zambian nationals to minister to their neighbors and hopes to fight the rampant malnutrition by mixing the main staple, mashed corn, with soy to give it more protein. And in what may seem like an unusual touch, Bailey has started a beauty shop.

"We did hair washing, we clipped their nails, we washed their feet, we trimmed hair, we gave the children baths and did little things like that," Bailey says. "We did this in each compound that we went to, then we ended the evening with worship and evangelism. The whole focus was to restore the image of God to Zambians."

Teams travel to Zambia annually. When she is in the United States, Bailey—who is Sekelela's executive director—makes future plans.

In April 2003, the organization will partner with the Texas-based international humanitarian ministry Heart for the World and California-based worship leader Tommy Walker to host a Heal Our Land tour that will feature practical ministry during the day and evangelistic crusades at night. Bailey also is fine-tuning a project that will link U.S. children with Zambians by asking the American youth to purchase $5 bowls of food that will feed a Zambian child for a week.

Ilnisky still feels like his efforts are like a teaspoon in an ocean, but he has watched God open incredible doors. When a Zambian contact called saying 100 acres of farmland were available for $25,000, Ilnisky told him Sekelela would provide the money, though he didn't know how. Within two weeks, every dollar had come in.

After Bailey was featured in the local newspaper for the work she was doing with Sekelela, a woman came to visit her and left a check for $10,000. On another occasion a man Ilnisky had known for years sent him a check for $30,000. Another stranger walked in their offices and handed them a check for $19,000, exceeding their $12,000 budget for medicine and food. Sekelela also has received thousands of clothing items and $700,000 worth of medical supplies.

"It's been absolutely miraculous," Ilnisky says. "It's been that way ever since we started this project."

These ordinary people from Florida have found that a teaspoon of hope goes a long way in Africa. On each visit, Bailey, a worship leader at Lighthouse, leads the children in singing inspirational songs she wrote. They are recorded on a CD titled *Sekelela* (Rejoice) Africa's Orphans that helps fund the ministry.

There is hardly a Zambian family that AIDS hasn't touched. Ilnisky says the young professionals are dying "like flies"—with life expectancy at 37 years—leaving the nation with an uncertain future. "In some parts of Africa...there's no such thing as a week that goes by that somebody—some neighbor, some friend, some-body you worked with—hasn't died from AIDS," he says.

Yet he and Bailey see past the dark clouds. "The children," Ilnisky says without hesitation, "are our only hope."

Adds Bailey: "The kids—these little, sometimes suffering kids—just have enough strength to turn their heads up and look at you...after you've just washed their hair...wanting to communicate: 'Thank you. Thank you for caring,'" Bailey says. "I think that's some of the moti-vating force that keeps me going. And recognizing that God has raised us up for such a time as this. And if we don't do it, who will?"

Bio
Adrienne S. Gaines is associate editor of Charisma and Ministries Today magazines. She wrote a cover story on Africa's AIDS crisis in March 2001.

15

A Light in Louisiana

Tonja Myles used to deal drugs and sell her body.
But after she found Jesus and launched a recovery program for addicts,
President Bush introduced her to the world as a hero.

BY ERNEST HERNDON

When Tonja Myles received an invitation to attend the State of the Union address in January, she was stunned. The former drug addict, prostitute and Satanist-turned-Christian considered it an extraordinary honor to receive a personal invite from the president of the United States.

When Myles arrived at the Capitol she was grateful just at the thought of getting a seat in the back row of the audience. She never imagined that she would be seated in the first lady's box and hear President Bush praise her Set Free Indeed ministry, calling it a prime example of a faith-based program.

"Our nation is blessed with recovery programs that do amazing work," Bush said. "One of them is found at the Healing Place Church in Baton Rouge, Louisiana. A man in the program said, 'God does miracles in people's lives, and you never think it could be you.'"

The president went on to encourage Americans to get involved. "Tonight, let us bring to all Americans who struggle with drug addiction this message of hope: The miracle of recovery is possible, and it could be you."

"I was just trying not to pass out on national TV," Myles recalls, closing her eyes and gritting her teeth to replay the moment. Afterward she met with the Bushes at a reception and received a bear hug from the president. Bush told her, "Tonja, we're so proud for what you do."

"I said, 'Thank you for the shout-out.' Then I thought, Lord, he may not even know what that is."

A shout-out is street slang for a word of praise. The difference in lingo seems to illustrate the vast cultural gap between a south Louisiana former drug dealer and an upper crust Texas politician, but to Myles there is no difference.

"He had a problem with alcohol and God set him free," she says of Bush. "And even though he's one of the most powerful people on Earth, his daughters have some problems with alcohol. So it affects everyone."

Officials even invited her back to participate in the White House Bible-study fellowship in early July.

"I count it an honor that they asked me to do it," she says. "Who would have thought that one day I'd be ministering at the White House?"

The visits to Washington cap off a story—or set of stories—about Myles' life. Healing Place Church, for instance, started 10 years ago with 12 people. Today it has 4,000 who are gearing up to build a 3,800-seat sanctuary.

The nondenominational church began when a benefactor gave pastor Dino Rizzo $400 to start a church and advised him: "Take care of the lost, the poor, the hurting. God will build the church."

Set Free Indeed is one of 48 ministries at the church. Myles, 39, and her husband, Darren, 36—a plumber by trade and an associate minister at the church—started the ministry with 10 to 20 people in 2002. Now, more than 100 people attend the Friday-night sessions. But the most improbable story of all, say folks who know her, is Tonja Myles.

"Tonja's just an incredible young lady," Rizzo says. "God has totally and radically changed her life—from the streets, drug addiction, several other tragic events in her life."

Her broken past now defines what she does for others. She spends her life—she and Darren—helping other people.

The ability to see beyond Bush's presidential luster to the personal problems he has undergone is characteristic of the Myleses. "They're not pretentious," Rizzo says. "Whether you're rich or poor, black or white, from the country club or curbside, they just draw everybody."

Dying a Spiritual Death

Tonja Myles was born and raised in Baton Rouge, Louisiana, an area Darren refers to as a "chemical plant and farm community." Her life, though, was anything but typical. She was molested at age 7, her mother was an alcoholic, and until Myles' conversion 17 years ago, life was a catastrophe.

Today, with a successful ministry and numerous accomplishments to her credit, it is hard to believe Myles abused drugs throughout high school and sold "uppers, downers, speed and coke" as a college student. Just one conversation with her, and it becomes obvious that the grace of God and her past failures in life are what qualify this woman to minister to people.

If a woman is struggling through the pain of abortion, Myles can help. Years ago she had two abortions, one from a man who introduced her to Satan worship.

When prostitutes need a way out, she can show them. She once heeded the advice of a friend and tried prostitution as a way to support her crack-cocaine habit.

"It's not like I stood on a corner, but a prostitute is a prostitute is a prostitute. I slept with married men and got money for drugs," she told Charisma.

At one point in her life, Myles says, she attempted to end it all with suicide. Though her memories of that moment are still foggy, she says she wound up at her grandmother's house hysterically insisting that "the devil" was trying to kill her. But as her grandmother began to pray, Myles allowed the Holy Spirit to turn things around. She made a vow to the Lord to dedicate the rest of her life "to helping others get set free."

"I always thought it was about religion and not about relationships, but it's not," she says. Holding true to her words, Myles developed a relationship with God and with others. Then she met Darren Myles.

"After the Lord, he's been the best thing that ever happened to me," she says. "He knew I was a new creature in Christ. He knew about my background."

The two come from different backgrounds. He was raised in north

Louisiana in a church family, had accepted God as a teenager and believed he was called to preach. Yet they hit it off as friends and fellow believers with a heart for ministry. Together they began preaching on street corners in "bad parts of town."

"We just went with a message of hope," Myles says, adding that people were generally receptive to them. Street corners weren't their only venue.

"We just began to minister in prison, nursing homes, anywhere people would have us," she recalls. "We always knew that deliverance and people being set free was what it was all about."

They preached at The Salvation Army (and still do), spoke in schools and canvassed neighborhoods in "the worst drug-infested areas of Baton Rouge," Myles says.

Her boldness wasn't confined to low places. She called the governor's office and managed to get funding for her efforts. She and Darren got corporate sponsors to provide prizes to give away at a "day in the park." Those prizes included free airline tickets—"airline tickets in the 'hood," she says with a chuckle.

As their ministry grew, Myles heard about pastor Rizzo and Healing Place Church. She approached him with an idea for a ministry to help addicts. The name Set Free Indeed comes from John 8:36, "'If the Son sets you free, you will be free indeed'" (NIV).

Transforming Lives

A little before 7 o'clock on a Friday evening, Tonja and Darren shut themselves into an office to pray while the Healing Place praise and worship team strike up mellow music in the 1,200-seat sanctuary.

People trickle in as slides show slogans such as: "Where will you spend eternity—smoking or nonsmoking?" and "Hell—Don't even go there." The slogans continue with messages that reach the heart. "LIFE: Live in Freedom Everyday"; "Wal-Mart isn't the only saving place"; "Jesus is my anti-drug"; "Don't give up if you mess up"; "We are called to stand out, not blend in"; "Jesus beat the devil with two sticks (a cross)"; "While faith makes all things possible, love makes it easier. We love you. The Set Free Indeed Ministry Team."

It's at meetings like this where people such as team leader Chuck Wallace get free from past problems. Wallace describes his sense of failure after losing a leadership position in a Baptist church because of his divorce.

"I partied, had a good time and tried to drown my sorrows," he tells the crowd. "But because God did not condemn me but pronounced me useful, I am able to stand before you tonight."

Then Myles addresses the audience: "Tonight we're going to renounce some of the root causes of why you've messed up." She holds up a poster with strips of paper bearing the words rejection, fear, pride, rebellion, anger, depression, self-doubt, deception, jealousy, unmet needs, unresolved issues, unhealed hurts.

She tears them away one by one, saying: "I don't care what you've done in the past. God will forgive you if you ask Him. God can heal you. He can set you free."

The audience divides into several groups. In one, about 20 men—black and white, rich and poor, young and old—cluster at the back of the sanctuary, talking about their problems, defeats and victories. One has been in prison five times and currently beds down at The Salvation Army. Another is a public official who's had problems with alcohol. One man has been substance-free for five years, another for 29 days, while one may be under the influence, judging by the way he keeps nodding off.

This night, a latecomer shows up, red-faced and distraught. This is a first-time meeting for him and he's suicidal, he says, because his girlfriend left. He spends his days in bed; he's let his business go; he's been in and out of the hospital. The group offers attention and sympathy, and the leader gives words of encouragement with information about follow-up help.

"It's all about helping somebody else, extending your hand, because when you start helping somebody else you help yourself as well," says Troy Cooper, a recovering cocaine and gambling addict who today is one of 25 Set Free Indeed volunteers. Cooper has tried other rehabilitation methods, and nothing has worked except reliance on the Lord and fellow Christians.

"People who have been in addiction know that time and time and time again you've tried to quit on your own and you can't do it," he says. "You've got to have a source, and this place is a source."

A Media Whirlwind

When a local newspaper reported on Myles' ministry, White House speechwriters read a quote made by a Set Free Indeed participant, and President Bush wanted to use it in his State of the Union address. Jim Towey, director of the White House Office of Faith-Based and Community Initiatives and assistant to the president, called Healing Place Church to confirm the quote. He wound up talking with Myles, and the rest is history.

"My attention quickly moved from the quote to the person because here she was, an individual who had bottomed out on the streets that had been lifted up by the Lord and was now spending her Friday nights with her husband trying to help other people while they ran a plumbing business," Towey says. "And I thought, This sounds like an exceptional woman."

As the date for the speech neared, officials asked Towey if he could recommend anyone to sit in Laura Bush's box during the State of the Union address.

"I thought of Tonja because she was the living embodiment of the faith-based initiative. ... President Bush has said repeatedly that his faith-based initiative is not about religion but results, and here was a woman whose life was turned around by the Lord and was now out there trying to turn other lives around," Towey says.

"Our lives changed just that fast," Myles says, snapping her fingers. "It was just like one big media event. ... It was the biggest media circus we ever saw."

From *The 700 Club* to *National Public Radio* to *The New York Times*, all types of news outlets sent reporters to interview her. "It's been mostly favorable, but there have been people who don't really care for the president, so they've tried to make us look bad to make him look bad," she says.

Americans United for Separation of Church and State protested, insisting Bush was promoting evangelical Christianity. One syndicated columnist called such programs "religious indoctrination dressed up as social welfare." But Rep. Sharon Weston Broome, D-Baton Rouge, disagreed.

"I think that they are a shining example of what can happen in a support or outreach group," she says of the Myleses. "They've had tremendous results, and they haven't really had any government funding. So, I think if they were afforded an opportunity to get a government grant, they could probably double or triple the results that they're getting.

"I've met people in their program, and they are getting results. It may not be the conventional approach, but they're getting results."

But Myles doesn't worry about the negatives. She is currently working with Louisiana state officials to develop a method of documenting those results. "This time next year when someone says, 'Can we see your documentation?' we'll say, 'Here you go,'" she says. "But the proof is in the changed lives."

Mike Duffy is one of those state officials she's working with. As acting deputy secretary for the Office of Addictive Disorder, he plans to contract with Myles to expand faith-based programs in Louisiana.

"We both are about attempting to help suffering people," Duffy says. "I support her ministry 100 percent—not financially, you understand, but I applaud her efforts to minister to those individuals who are struggling with addiction."

As Set Free Indeed progresses, Duffy expects it will include leaders with state credentials, such as licensed clinical social workers or board-certified substance-abuse counselors. Duffy says he sees no conflict in using a religious program to treat addicts.

"Those of us who are involved in the provision of treatment throughout this country recognize that without a spiritual element— and we're certainly not defining that spiritual element—there in fact is no real recovery," he says.

Yet, Myles cites statistics that show most churches in the nation lack drug-addiction recovery ministries. One positive result of the media spotlight is that many have contacted her for help in starting one. She and Darren are devising a manual to help operate such programs.

Set Free Indeed is not a 12-step program, and it's not just for drug addicts, Myles says. Though she's not opposed to 12-step programs, she says they originate from biblical principles, so why not go to the source?

Set Free Indeed offers help to anyone who is physically or spiritually bound, whether by drugs, alcohol, pornography, gambling, depression, anger, homosexuality or other problems.

Having been in the grips of more than one such evil herself, Myles is a prime example of a seemingly hopeless life transformed by the power of God.

"I tell people I went from the crack house to the White House, from the gutter to greatness," she says. Though media attention may come and go, she is determined to follow through on the vow she made to God when He rescued her from the jaws of hell: "I'll die— I mean it—getting people set free."

Bio
Ernest Herndon is religion editor for the McComb, Mississippi, Enterprise-Journal. He is the author of numerous books, including Nature Trails and Gospel Tales: Stories of Grace From the Wilds of Mississippi, *due out in spring 2004 from InterVarsity Press.*

16

A Generous Soul in Chicago

Eddie R. Martin, a 75-year-old pastor with a small congregation and no salary, has fed more than 100 people a week for the last five years.

BY KIM R. ANDERSON

Collard greens, pinto beans, corn bread, string beans. Soul food. Stick-to-your-ribs cuisine. It's the kind of food the Rev. Eddie R. Martin, pastor of Mount Carmel Ridge Baptist Church in the inner city of Chicago, serves every Wednesday to more than 100 people in desperate need of nourishment.

He knows people need food for the soul, too. That's why before the long line forms and lunch is served, the men and women sit in the church's pews and listen to a Bible study usually taught by the founding pastor's wife, Rosie Harris, 82. After Harris ministers to the guests' spiritual needs, they dig into the food prepared by Martin and his dedicated team of volunteers.

Many of the people who come for lunch are facing hard times caused by unfortunate circumstances or poor choices. Some are homeless; others are drug addicts or prostitutes. Some just can't make ends meet. Attendance is usually higher at the end of the month when food stamps have run out. The predominantly African American neighborhood where the church is located has a high unemployment rate, and the annual income for a family of five averages $12,000-$14,000.

In the five years that Martin, 75, has led the feeding ministry, he and his team have not missed serving a weekly meal, despite their limited funding. The local food pantry supplies some of the food, and the 107 church members give what they can to support the outreach. But a good portion of the money for food and supplies comes out of Martin's own pocket, and he draws no salary from the church.

"It's not easy, but God is good," Martin says. "The neighborhood changes, and people come and go, but I enjoy being able to help somebody. I've learned how to treat people. I've never had to call the police on anyone. All my trust is in the Lord."

Growing up in Georgia with seven brothers and one sister, Martin developed faith in God at an early age. His whole family was involved in church, and God was an important part of his life as a young boy. After graduating from high school, Martin served in the Army and fought in the Korean War. After settling in Chicago, he worked in the construction industry as a labor superintendent until his retirement 20 years ago.

Martin sensed God calling him into full-time ministry more than five years ago, though he lacked formal ministry training or a seminary degree. He believes "God makes the ministers, not schools." The schooling he does receive week after week as pastor of an urban church is a lesson in trust and total dependence on God, knowing that He is the only one who can help people in desperate need.

As a participant in the African American Fellowship, a network of 108 Chicago pastors who support one another and receive ministry training, Martin is highly esteemed by other ministers.

"Rev. Martin has done a magnificent job with the feeding ministry," says pastor Edward Clark of Good Hope Baptist Church and president of the fellowship. "He has made a difference in his community. People who don't have food and might be tempted to steal food to live now have a ministry to go to."

In addition to the outreach on Wednesdays, Martin cares for 10 senior citizens in the church's neighborhood. He delivers meals to them and helps in any way he can. He also feeds two families in need of assistance every Sunday after church. He collects clothing donations for them, too, and offers help with housing needs.

"Rev. Martin is a lighthouse in the neighborhood," says Tom Kleinfeldt, church development director of the Chicago Metropolitan Baptist Association. "Others may see the people around his church as subhuman due to their rough lifestyle, but Rev. Martin shows kindness to the people he serves. He is an oasis and light for people living in darkness."

Helping him to be a light are the faithful volunteers, including his wife of 15 years, Frances, and Alice Randle, who show up week after week to prepare and serve the food. Despite being diagnosed with bone cancer eight years ago and receiving chemotherapy treatments twice a week, Randle says her deep love for Jesus Christ motivates her to minister to the poor, no matter what.

"It's a blessing to be a blessing," she says. "The people we serve just need to be loved, and they need Jesus. The Lord has placed me here. I'm thankful I can be a part of it. It's so fulfilling to make a difference in someone's life. This church is in a strategic location for church work."

And there's plenty of work to do. In addition to the feeding ministry, Martin preaches every Sunday to a congregation that has grown from just three members five years ago to more than 100 today.

"Anything you like to do, you don't mind doing it," says Martin, who has 16 children and is a grandfather, great-grandfather and great-great-grandfather. "I can't sit around. When I wake up, I have to move. I'm usually up at 3 a.m. with my coffee, studying the Bible and getting my message ready for Sunday."

Martin's first message at Mount Carmel came from James 2, focusing on verse 26: "As the body without the spirit is dead, so faith without deeds is dead" (NIV). The message came alive when the feeding ministry started soon after.

Not allowing his age, limited resources or a challenging environment to deter him from making a difference in people's lives, Martin offers his community a tangible expression of his faith in Christ. Using the resources he has, Martin has seen lives turn around. Each year he baptizes more than a dozen men and women who not only had their physical needs met, but also their hunger for a relationship with God.

The way Martin sees it, that's real food for the soul.

Bio
Kim R. Anderson is a freelance writer and author of several books. She and her husband, Eric, have two daughters and live in Algonquin, Illinois.

For more information about Eddie R. Martin's feeding ministry, write to Mount Carmel Ridge Baptist Church 7326 S. Halsted St., Chicago, IL 60621; or call (773) 483-5067. Send tax-deductible contributions to Christian Life Missions, P.O. Box 952248, Lake Mary, FL 32795-2248.

17

A Rich Woman In the 'Hood

Dorothy Moore grew up in a world of chauffeurs,
debutante balls and fine china. Today, she's helping drug
addicts and single moms in the worst parts of Dallas.

By Carol Chapman Stertzer

Throughout east Dallas, rows of run-down family businesses and
dilapidated houses represent years of hopelessness and neglect.
A quick-fix solution seems out of reach for many business owners
and families. However, an unlikely crusader began targeting this
community for good 16 years ago, and her efforts are paying off.
Gang-related violence is down, the neighborhood schools are
improving, and crack houses have been converted into homes for
adults who are trying to change.

As president of Reconciliation Outreach, 66-year-old Dorothy Moore
is living proof that God can use anyone to make a difference in the
'hood, as she affectionately calls it. She left a life of luxury years ago
and has no regrets. In fact, in inner-city missions Moore says she
has found true happiness and her reason for being.

Moore's upbringing hardly prepared her to work with the underprivi-
leged. Her father, Harold Engh, made it through only eighth grade,
but he quickly achieved the American dream by becoming president of the wire and cable company where he had once worked
scrubbing floors.

Moore grew up in New York having her own chauffeur, chef and
nanny. Her mother hired staff who had worked for prominent families so she could learn how to buy the socially appropriate silver
and china.

During summers the Engh family spent time in Sycamore, Illinois,
where Moore's parents had been raised. Later, her father bought
a company in Sycamore, and Moore attended school there for a
couple of years.

"The chauffeur would take me to school, and I'd make him drop me off two blocks from school so the other kids wouldn't see him," recalls Moore, who didn't want to be so different from her classmates.

As a teen, she went to a prestigious boarding school for girls and became a New York debutante. She studied opera in college before turning her attention to philosophy and psychology.

Despite her privileged upbringing, Moore gained a heart of compassion for others. "I think all my life I identified with people who had pain or lack," she says.

In her early years, she would listen to their household staff talk about life's difficulties. When she traveled from New York to Illinois, staff members Jonas and Cora couldn't go into most restaurants because of their skin color. "That offense stuck with me strongly," she says.

After college Moore moved to San Diego. There she worked for a radio station as a talk-show host and sang on the side. Although she dated sometimes, she wasn't smitten until she met Bob Moore, a Navy lieutenant from west Texas.

"He was everything that a Texan should have been," she says. "I had dated lots of boys who were caught up in social things and money. I really wanted a man whom I could respect the way I respected my father."

The couple dated about six months and married in 1959. Because of their cultural differences, those early years were difficult. "You don't change a spoiled brat overnight into somebody that learns to be a servant," she admits about herself.

Experiencing God

After Bob graduated from the University of Texas Law School in Austin, the Moores spent a couple of years in Chicago. In 1974, Bob got an offer to work for an oil company in Dallas—and the timing couldn't have been better.

Having gotten close to filing for divorce because of family problems, Dorothy was invited to a Christian seminar. She went—and experienced a life change.

"I got on my knees and made a commitment to Christ," she says. "I had a total transformation and became deeply in love with Jesus."

Moore immersed herself in the Bible and was closely discipled by a friend for four years. She joined Highland Park Presbyterian (an affluent church that has been very supportive of her inner-city work).

In 1975 Bob was asked to take a position in Houston. When the couple moved, Moore felt like she had lost everything. "I was taken out of a cocoon of love and training to a whole new situation. I was miserable," she says.

Together they began attending St. Andrews Presbyterian Church, where there was openness to the gifts of the Holy Spirit. Though skeptical of the spiritual gifts at first, Moore says she "began to see that these people who were Spirit-filled were accomplishing things that were important." She too wanted whatever the Holy Spirit had in store for her.

Moore continued to grow spiritually, and within 10 years she was teaching, speaking in churches and serving as president of a Houston chapter Aglow International that was trying to bring about racial reconciliation.

In 1985, the Moores moved back to Dallas, and they quickly got involved at Hillcrest Church, a nondenominational congregation of about 5,000 attendees today, pastored by Morris Sheets.

About a year after they returned to Dallas, Moore joined a team to pray in the inner city of east Dallas near downtown. Based on the group's research, the area they had chosen had the highest crime rate in the city.

There the group set up a couple of tents: one for the adults, the other for kids. Cambodian and Spanish translators were on hand. Within four days, Moore says, the group had attracted a large crowd.

One night when Moore was speaking, some Asian Americans came forward to receive Christ. She motioned for help from the Cambodian translator, who quickly discovered these were Vietnamese, not Cambodians.

"We started to pray," Moore says, "and for the first time in my life, this nasal language came out of me. I began to speak in an Oriental tongue, and the kids began to cry. They could understand what I was saying."

After two weeks of tent ministry in east Dallas, the growing inner-city group became known as the East Dallas Crusaders for Christ. Sensing a need for a permanent presence in the inner city, Moore incorporated Reconciliation Outreach in 1987.

Rather than plant a church in the inner city, Moore decided to send the locals to Hillcrest every Sunday for training and discipleship. Hillcrest fully supported the decision. "This has been an effective way for the two groups of people to come together in relationships," she says, "and it has supported me so I didn't just get down there and die."

Not surprisingly, there have been a few incidents with the children.

"You can't take a child who has never been taught to say please and thank you and expect them to suddenly become nice, well-behaved church kids," she says. "They will offend people. They will act in ways that are inappropriate in a north Dallas church.

"We've had some things happen that have been funny and some not so funny," she adds. "But it has been healthy on both sides and brought a lot of friendship across the lines."

According to Sheets, Moore is a visionary who is carrying out her God-given plan. "The dispossessed of Dallas are receiving emergency help and training through Reconciliation Outreach," he says.

Feeling the need to establish a strong spiritual presence in the community, Moore launched an inner-city church in January.

"We still need the relationship with the suburban church and will continue to have it," she explains, "but the sense of needing a church planted here in the inner city is very strong for us. Plus, getting 150 people in cars and buses every week gets to be very complicated."

A 'Holy Ghost Clean-Out'

For the first 10 years in east Dallas, Moore focused on youth ministry. Early on, she was amazed at the hunger these kids had for God and how free they felt to worship. "I think it was the first safe place many of these kids found where they could express what they felt and not be called sissies," she says.

About five years ago, Moore began to build the adult program. Through generous donations from charities and foundations, the ministry has bought several run-down houses where drug deals previously took place. Volunteers from area churches and corporations such as UPS, FedEx and AT&T have helped repair the buildings and make them livable.

Two ministry homes, each with housemothers, are designed for women who are trying to get on their feet. Many of them have been addicted to drugs; others have been abused and need a safe harbor. Reconciliation Outreach also has three men's houses, a children's building and a day-care center. A new building containing 19 apartments is for individuals and families who need housing assistance until they can support themselves.

Chapel is held every Monday, Wednesday and Friday at noon and at night. Willie Burnette leads many of the services and does a lot of the pastoring. Other programs offered at Reconciliation Outreach include share groups, personal-growth groups, prison ministry, after-school programs and business-skills classes. For many participants, one-on-one prayer time is critical.

"Most of these kids and adults live under what I call the 'curse of generations,'" says Moore, who is involved in inner-healing and deliverance ministry at Hillcrest Church. She has presented her "Breaking Generational Curses" seminar in churches throughout Texas and in India, Romania and Indonesia.

"You don't just put the gospel on top of other things. Many of these people have to have a 'Holy Ghost clean-out,' if you will. Then the gospel takes its rightful place and becomes the foundation of life itself for them," she explains.

Women who live in the homes are required to gather for prayer every day at 6 a.m.; the men meet earlier to accommodate their work schedules. "We take them in our own vehicles to job sites," Moore says. "That way the employers know they are safe in hiring them." Reconciliation Outreach also provides drug-testing as an incentive to potential employers.

Moore acknowledges that it is difficult for inner-city residents to find jobs—partly because of the current recessionary economy but also because most of them are undereducated and underqualified, and some have criminal records.

"There are all kinds of reasons for an employer not to hire them," she points out, "so we do everything we can—both in the spiritual and in the natural—to qualify them for jobs."

Changing East Dallas

As Reconciliation Outreach continues to purchase neighborhood property, this community can't help but change. "You don't bring the presence of Christ and the body of Christ into a neighborhood without changing it," Moore believes.

Approximately 80 percent of those who have gone through the organization's six-month and one-year programs stay clean and are able to enter the real world. "It's a long interview process to qualify," she says, "and they are given every opportunity to make it."

In 1999, Sen. Kay Bailey Hutchison of Texas honored Moore with an Unsung Heroines Award. She also has received a Dallas Independent School District award for her work with the district's alternative program.

To prepare participants to live responsibly and more self-sufficiently, the staff of Reconciliation Outreach teaches them how to manage money and requires they establish a savings program so they will have money to take with them when they leave. They are also taught about such things as good health and nutrition.

"Some of the people who have gone through our program may stay close to us for the rest of their lives, but many go back to their homes and families," Moore says. "We've had lots of homes restored, and a lot of children brought back to single moms who had been farmed out to Grandma. We teach the mother how to parent and the child how to get over some of the fears and abuse that went on in the homes before the parent came into the program."

Moore started Reconciliation Outreach with $5,000. Today the annual budget exceeds $700,000. She says "public relations and being visible" make a difference in keeping the ministry alive. She also stresses the importance of building the trust of supporters.

"If people are going to give you money, you have to have an absolutely clean record. We use the same accounting methods that Billy Graham does, and they are gone over with a fine-tooth comb by the same people who do his books," she says.

Reconciliation Outreach has eight full-time staff members. Other employees work on a stipend basis and receive free on-site housing.

Administrator Jacqueline Lucas went through the program almost four years ago. She didn't have drug problems; she just needed spiritual peace. "I had everything I needed, but I was the most miserable person in the world," she says.

"When I first went into the program, I thought, What is a woman like Dorothy doing down here?" admits 36-year-old Lucas. She quickly saw that Moore ,though firm, has a tender heart for helping others.

Although Moore hasn't named a successor, two of her four children are involved in the ministry. Holly, who has a master's degree in reading disabilities, works at the organization's day-care center and tutors students. Clay oversees the ministry's outdoor market, which contains new and donated items for raising funds and is a source of jobs for residents. Moore's husband, a Dallas attorney, provides legal advice.

Almost 500 volunteers—many from local churches—work for the ministry in a year. Moore estimates that people from more than 50 churches helped in 2002. Internships also are available.

In addition to her inner-city ministry, Moore is active in the community. Dallas is filled with churches that have strong programs, but Moore sees a need for reconciliation across denominational lines. Despite her full schedule, Moore shows no signs of slowing down.

"I think the whole concept of retirement is so far away from what the Scriptures teach," she says. "The more you grow in Christ, the more you want to serve Him...doing whatever He asks.'

As long as God wants her involved in missions work, Moore will be there. "I love what I do—I'm probably happier now than I've ever been in my life," she says.

While noting that life isn't pain-free for anyone, Moore wishes others could have the joy she has found. "I cannot guarantee others of being happy or always having the good life, but I would like to help them find the same joy I've found just by living Christianity," she says. "It's living it every day in such a way that you go home and feel satisfied."

Bio
Carol Chapman Stertzer is a Dallas-based correspondent for Charisma.

18

A Tender Warrior In South Dakota

Jerry Yellowhawk has spent his life trying to reach the Lakota Indians.
His goal now is to translate the Bible into his native tongue.

By John L. Moore

Jerry Yellowhawk is no longer a clean-cut Native American pastor
who wears a dark suit, white shirt and black tie. That is how he
dressed in the 1960s, when he posed for the cover of a gospel
album with a guitar in hand and his wife, Johanna, at his side.

Today, at age 66, Yellowhawk looks more comfortable. His raven-
black ponytail—without a trace of gray—reaches down his back.
He wears Wranglers, boots and T-shirts with brightly colored Native
designs.

He is no longer trying to fit the white man's mold of what a
Christian should look like.

Yellowhawk is a quiet man. Like many Native Americans of his
generation, he is disinclined to talk about himself. In fact, until his
deep, dark eyes have had time to appraise your soul, he is reticent
to talk much at all. You sense he simply wants to be about the
Lord's business, and that means reaching his people, the Lakota
Sioux, by any means possible.

Raised on the Cheyenne River Indian Reservation in South Dakota,
Yellowhawk accepted Christ in a Wesleyan Methodist church when
he was 18. Six years later he graduated from the David Brainerd
Memorial Bible College—a campus site that would later cause a
haunting in his life—and became an assistant pastor in Pierre,
South Dakota.

In 1966 he pioneered a church, Cheyenne River Lakota Chapel,
and pastored it for 18 years. The church is now pastored by Danny
LaPlante while Yellowhawk dedicates himself to translating the Bible

into the Lakota language. (He is two years into a project with support from the American Bible Society and Wycliffe Bible Translators.) He also helps organize strategic Christian gatherings of indigenous peoples.

With more than 40 years of Christian service behind him—almost all of it as a pastor and missions leader in the Wesleyan Methodist church—Yellowhawk now stands at a crossroads. There is a pain in his past, caused by racism and hurtful misunderstandings from both secular society and the church. And he feels his future is undefined.

"Jerry is changing how we think about Native ministry," says Native Christian leader Richard Twiss, who counts Yellowhawk as a mentor. "His goal is to move the Native work away from a missions model to a culturally sensitive approach to ministry."

This new approach—called "cultural contextualization" by many— has prompted criticism from both white and Native branches of the church because Yellowhawk attends secular native powwows as well as Native Sacred Assemblies where cultural dress and music are used as expressions of Christian worship. The long hair, buck-skins, headdresses and drums unsettle some.

"You would think 40 years of ministry would mean something," says Yellowhawk, who is bothered by the suspicion and condemnation his unconventional work brings. "But if you mention 'dance' or 'drums,' some people get nervous."

"Jerry is an elder," explains Adrian Jacobs, an Iroquois-Cayuga from Ontario, who worked with Yellowhawk on the Wesleyan Native American Missions Board. "It is not the Lakota way for elders to impose themselves on anyone," he adds, noting that Yellowhawk "did everything the denominational church wanted him to do."

Jacobs, now an outreach worker with LAMP, the Lutheran Association of Missionaries and Pilots, explains some of his mentor's pain: "He cut his hair, he wore a suit and tie, he preached three-point sermons and sang hymns, but his heart remained unassimilated. His heart remained with the Lakota people."

That love for his people is one of the few things Yellowhawk will talk about. He earnestly desires to bring the love of Jesus to the Sioux and knows it may take the Native culture and Scripture in Native language to do it.

Assisted by Rosalie Little Thunder, he works several days a week translating the Bible into the Lakota dialect. "It is very exhausting work. I get weary. Sometimes I just need to get away and dance for a while," he says, explaining how powwows help to keep him physically fit and peaceful.

Jacobs also explains how he and Jerry had a dream to purchase the Brainerd Bible School campus when it was offered for sale and to start a First Nations Institute. Instead, through a series of events, the campus was sold to The Nature Conservancy and the chance for a Native training center in their sacred Black Hills vanished.

The loss of land reopens wounds that run many generations deep, but Yellowhawk is warrior-stoic on the matter. If he has been wounded by injustice he does not voluntarily show his scars.

"Jerry is a model of quiet strength and determination to hold to his convictions," says Mike Jacobs (no relation to Adrian), a Native worship leader and musician. "He has always taught us that you don't trade one sin-stained culture for another to be a Christian."

If Yellowhawk looks back with regret, he doesn't cast stones at his former denomination or a white church that misunderstood him. Instead, he regrets his own former legalism. His rigid rules of conduct at home (including a strict policy forbidding any work on Sunday) and his earlier detachment from Lakota culture distanced him from two of his three children.

His son, well-known Native artist James Yellowhawk, is a believer. But his married twin daughters are not—reminding him why so many Native youth have rejected what they call "white man's religion."

Still, in his quiet way, Yellowhawk continues on—marching to the beat of his very different drum. He has, after all, an entire Bible to translate and a host of young Native Christian warriors to mentor.

Bio
John L. Moore writes Western novels and lives in Miles City, Montana.

19

An Angel of Mercy in the Desert

She's 87, but her age hasn't stopped Agnes Numer from feeding the world's poor from her makeshift ministry base in rural California.

BY STEVEN LAWSON

Agnes Numer has much in common with Moses. She spends lots of time in the desert, looks to the heavens for "manna" for her people and has never written a letter of appeal asking for help. While Moses led the Jewish people out of captivity into the promised land, "Sister Agnes," as she's nicknamed, plucks the poor out of poverty and directs them toward God's promises.

Scores of needy people regard her as another Mother Teresa. She is to them the unsung provider of their next meal, their advocate for medical treatment, even their teacher of lessons on husbandry. Ironically, though she once had a personal meeting with Pope John Paul II and has been honored by President Bush, most of the people she aids do not even know her name. To them, she is simply a rescuer, their hero.

At age 87, she operates her Sommer Haven ministry from a cluster of salvaged mobile homes in the Mojave Desert of California. Her land has been designated for an international airport, but for now it's her headquarters from which she quietly directs her unorthodox aid and redevelopment agency and its all-volunteer force of about 60.

Together, they touch distant outposts that include Indonesia, Israel, Nigeria, Cambodia, as well as the state of Nagaland, India, and the U.S. Navajo Indian nation. Sommer Haven sends out about 10 cargo-sized containers of food and medical supplies a year, and sponsors training centers, dispatches missionaries and runs literacy programs. The ministry maintains full-time schools in Mexico, the Philippines and Palmdale, California.

In Southern California alone, it supplies 52 smaller ministries (food banks, churches and the like) weekly with staples, canned goods, medicine and whatever else comes in from a loose and growing network of donors. Sister Agnes and her headquarters staff also assist about 60 walk-ins a day.

"Money means nothing to me except to give it," Sister Agnes says. "God could put untold riches into my hands, but it would only be to meet the needs of the world."

Born in a small Ohio town, Sister Agnes knew poverty early. Her mother died when Agnes was 11, two years before the Great Depression began. Postponing her education, Agnes spent five years taking care of her siblings and learning to grow food, a lesson she would later teach in impoverished nations. At 16, hardened and bitter, she accepted Jesus as her Savior at a Methodist tent-revival meeting after being invited by her mailman.

Life was never again the same. She says that soon after her conversion God planted in her a desire to take the gospel to Africa, India and China. At age 18, God told her, "As I was with Moses, so I will be with you," she adds. She did not fully realize at the time that His promise to her would first mean 40 years of training, then—after she had married and raised her family—40 years of ministry, so far.

"God has told me I will pass over 100 years and not die," a still vigorous Sister Agnes says between sips of green tea. She gave up caffeine years ago because it made her heart jumpy. "I don't feel any age. A little pain, yes, but no age. My ministry has not really even begun yet."

She moved to Southern California in the 1940s and was baptized in the Holy Spirit at a Foursquare church. Ten years later, she relocated to Palmdale and has been there since. All along, she has led small prayer and Bible-study groups and reached out to the poor.

It wasn't until 1976 that her ministry went international. She traveled to Nigeria and preached in remote villages. In one place she spent five hours instructing a pastor and his people on how to stand in prayer and fasting against communism, which, at the time, threatened to envelop the region.

As she returned home, she realized that it had been exactly 40 years since she received her first word from God about Moses. Soon she was off to India, where she ministered to Roman Catholic charismatics, received specific words from God and gained an ingrained passion for the poor of Bombay and beyond.

In Southern California, Sister Agnes and some volunteers ran vacation Bible schools and took bread to the Navajo Indians, later expanding to reach out to the Blackfoot in Montana.

The food distribution began in Sister Agnes' Palmdale neighborhood and was funded by money from an insurance policy. Local residents Ray Loya and his sons were collecting cans, trying to gather enough to exchange for a meal. The Sommer Haven team reached out to them. Today Loya volunteers as Sommer Haven's director of distribution, and his daughter, Tery, who at age 11 was a streetwise alcoholic, is married and works in full-time ministry.

Sister Agnes' initial impulse was to found Sommer Haven according to an established ministry model. "But God told me it would not be that way," she says—although the ministry does operate with a board of directors and follow full accountability guidelines. "He said to go to the markets and tell them what we were doing."

She did. Since then, markets, packinghouses, distributors, growers, food banks and even one local meat market have donated. "It is not unusual to see tractor trailers come in here with full loads," says Sommer Haven volunteer Kathleen Thomas.

"I believe God will use America to feed the world," Sister Agnes adds. "There are many wealthy ranchers...and food manufacturers. They just need the vision."

Sommer Haven has never asked directly for contributions. Instead, Sister Agnes relies on faith. "As the needs are revealed," she says, "God meets them."

Sister Agnes recalls one need in particular. God had told her to give 13 people $1,000 each. Problem was, she did not have $13,000. She had not told anyone about God's direction, but an unmarked envelope with $13,000 inside was delivered to Sommer Haven. One of the $1,000 recipients, a group Sister Agnes had worked with in India, later told her that when they received the money they were down to their last meal and on the brink of dissolving the ministry.

Sister Agnes and her volunteers are now in the process of acquiring new headquarters and warehousing property in the Palmdale area. They have large tracts of donated land that will be used for developmental training farms in Cambodia, China and Israel, but they are awaiting the finances to begin operations. In the meantime, Sister Agnes prepares for new ministry training classes.

"God took a little housewife, who did not get to finish college, to give the world a vision for the lost," Kathy Van Zandt, who's been with Sommer Haven for 22 years and is director of its school, says about Sister Agnes. "She has shown me that the Christian life is not only reading the Bible, singing and going to church, but it is realizing that Christ in us must be poured out of us to the world."

Bio
Steven Lawson is a former news editor for Charisma. He now lives in Los Angeles.

For more information, write Sommer Haven, P.O. Box 525, Littlerock, CA 93543; or log on at www.sommerhaven.com. Send tax-deductible contributions to Christian Life Missions, P.O. Box 952248, Lake Mary, FL 32795-2248.

20

God's Beacon Of Hope in Houston

By Jimmy Stewart

Bob Ferguson started a treatment program six years ago that has helped countless addicts kick harmful habits.

Come Friday afternoons, and Bob Ferguson is ready to pack his tackle, hitch his boat and roar off solo in his truck for a weekend of fishing. There's hardly anything he likes better. Hardly.

"I'm a fishing fiend," the 46-year-old Texas native says, drawing out his last word for a convincing emphasis.

Sometimes, after a long week of driving his wrecker truck and managing his West University Towing business in Houston, he might even pitch camp at his favorite spot and excuse himself from a Sunday morning church service. But only after he OKs it with his pastor of the last several years, Doug Stringer of Turning Point Christian Center (TPCC).

"On those days I just go to 'The Church of the Holy Mackerel,'" Ferguson quips, revealing a good-natured laugh.

Being a lone weekend angler is about the best thing this side of heaven to Ferguson. But he says he'd give it all up for the real heaven on earth that comes from being a fisher of men. He loves nothing better than to reel in people who are strung out on drugs or otherwise hopelessly hooked by personal defeats and introduce them to Jesus.

He does that every week through a citywide support group in Houston called Jesus in the Steps, which meets on Tuesdays from 7:30 p.m. till 9 p.m. at TPCC. Jesus in the Steps is primarily for drug addicts and alcoholics in all stages of recovery or addiction, but Ferguson emphasizes that no one is excluded from the group.

"It's good for anybody struggling with any kind of sin—whether it's drugs, alcohol, codependency, pornography, workaholism, homosexuality, sexual stuff. Doesn't matter," he says. "It's even good for the kooks in church who keep running around the same old mountain."

The program he founded six years ago and has held every Tuesday since is based on the 12 steps of recovery used by Alcoholics Anonymous (AA)—with one key exception. Ferguson prefers, instead of pointing people to an anonymous "higher power" advocated by AA, to plainly tell participants that only Jesus is capable of giving them a restored life.

"I lift Him up. He said if He was lifted up, He'd draw the people to Him. The Word of God breaks the yoke," he says. "He's a good God, and He desires to set them free."

Ferguson is no purveyor of a hope-so message. His ministry is experience-born, an extension of his own life that joins his love for people with his own freedom from a 10-year addiction to heroin, methadone and alcohol.

In 1987, when he was at the lowest point of his addiction after the death of his father, he injected enough heroin to get two people high. The overdose was intentional, meant to kill him.

He waited in his apartment for the narcotic coma to take control. The drugs knocked him out, but he regained consciousness a day later, sprawled across his bathroom floor. Instead of trying a second time, he went to Narcotics Anonymous.

It took two more years for him to get clean and sober. About that time, two of his friends whom he jokingly calls "nut cases" had become Christians and were attending TPCC. Ferguson witnessed a dramatic change in their lives and accepted their invitation to a Friday night service being taught by Stringer.

"I knew there was truth there, so I just kept going back on Fridays," he says. He kept going—for eight weeks—until Stringer finished his series on the work of the cross with a gritty message about how Jesus suffered for sin.

"It broke my heart when I heard about Jesus being crucified. I went running to the altar, and I have been running after Him ever since."

The running turned into fishing for lives when God spoke to him during a 40-day period of fasting and prayer in 1996 and gave him the idea for a program that joined the 12 steps with the Bible and total dependence on God.

A short time later his Tuesday night meeting was born. His format is quite simple—he teaches one of the 12 steps each week and relies on the Holy Spirit to accomplish everything else.

"I tell them all that it's not about where you've been—it's about where you're going," Ferguson says. "I just follow the Holy Spirit."

He opens every meeting with prayer. Then, using the Serenity New Testament for 12-step recovery, available at Christian bookstores and used by AA, he calls on people to read the verse for the night and comment.

"They can talk about anything they want to talk about for five minutes," he says. "I preach sometimes. If I do, I preach the cross."

He encourages group participation but doesn't require it. He finishes by reading an entry from the classic daily devotional My Utmost for His Highest by Oswald Chambers and closes the same way he opens. He says that anyone who wishes "prayer for salvation or to get free from sin" is encouraged to see him after the meeting.

Friends of Ferguson's in other areas of Houston lead three spin-off groups hosted by churches other than TPCC. One is directed by two women he led to Christ who formerly were lesbians and drug addicts. They conduct weekly meetings for residents of a halfway house in an area of the city known for its homeless kids and homosexual community.

The other is led by another friend whom he mentored in the faith. "Five years ago, he was a crack addict—just another guy on the street who, to look at, you would've thought there's no hope for him. Now, he's a main usher in the church, too." A third meeting is held at another local church.

As for his own past, it doesn't tempt him anymore, he says. "Another person from another time" is how he describes himself in his drug-induced days. "I found the love I've always been looking for. I don't need to shoot the dope I used to do."

Being now 46 years old and unmarried is probably his main struggle these days, he adds. But he says he's "98 percent free" of that one, thanks to being mentored by the Christian Men's Network and being accountable to Stringer and other men at TPCC. They keep him focused on God's calling.

Call it irony or God's plan, but in that calling Ferguson the fisherman found the hook that has snagged him for a life of service to Jesus.

"There is nothing like seeing someone pray for the first time to receive Jesus," Ferguson says. "Nothing compares with that. I can't put it into words. If that isn't God's will, I don't know what is."

He still gets excited when he thinks of where he's come from and how churches have embraced his hope for the addicted. His dream is that Jesus in the Steps will grow and more churches will want to host a group.

"Instead of fishing on weekends, I would rather travel around to start other groups," he says, and then adds: "I don't do this for recognition. I was a heroin addict. I was a character. I was mean— real hard. It took Jesus to change me. I wouldn't be anybody if it hadn't been for Jesus. I'm just a regular guy who got radically saved."

Bio
Jimmy Stewart is managing editor of Charisma.

21

How One Woman Took Hope to Haiti

Danita Estrella left a comfortable home and fulfilling career to
care for forgotten children in a Haitian orphanage.

By Mary Hutchinson

If anyone had an excuse not to be a missionary, it was Danita
Estrella. She was young, single, a woman, broke and inexperi-
enced in missions work.

But tomorrow morning, Danita, 36, will wake up to the sounds of
happy children rising for their day in one of the poorest areas in
Haiti—the poorest nation in the Western Hemisphere. She'll lie on
her bunk bed and stare at the ceiling a few inches from her face
as the children whisper and giggle down the hall. She will awaken
more than a missionary. She is a mother—to almost 30.

Alone, she has started the Hope for Haiti orphanage.

Her story began as a happy little girl raised in a Christian home.
Then when her parents divorced, she began to question the faith
she was reared in.

"I moved to California and lived the good life. I had the fancy car,
lovely apartment and glamorous job doing promotional modeling.
Then my life crashed again, and I found myself running back to the
Lord."

She moved back to Florida and became active in church work. "I
had been living for the Lord for almost 10 years, and I began to feel
very unsettled. Though I was part of a wonderful ministry at Without
Walls International Church in Tampa, Florida, I felt there had to be
more that God wanted me to do," she recalls.

"As a child my father had taken me to Haiti, and when I got a
chance to go there on a short medical mission, I knew something
was happening. When the trip was over, I found myself anxious to
return to Haiti. Two months later, I packed my bags and moved to
Haiti alone."

Danita sought out a work she could help. She found it in the local church and in a concrete block building that was home to a Christian school in the heart of Ouanaminthe, Haiti.

"The condition the children lived in around this school broke my heart. They wandered the streets naked all day. This town has no running water, no electricity, no phones... [and] no jobs.

"The people are hungry, survival is all they know. They leave their children alone all day to try to get food and water. Some parents go to the Dominican Republic in search of a better life ...and abandon these poor children."

Danita spent the first few months without clear direction from God. Then it happened: "I was eating alone in an open-air restaurant when I noticed the homeless children watching the customers eat. One little boy came close to my table and was watching me carefully, trying to position himself to grab whatever food I had left over.

"I looked into his soft brown eyes, and I couldn't give him my leftovers. I told him to wait; I wanted to buy him his own meal." As Danita turned to place the order, a man charged the little one with a huge whip. "The man used the same whip he had been herding cattle with to beat this small, helpless child!

"For a moment, I froze. The screams of the child could be heard up the street. In a spilt second, I was out of my chair and on that man. The people on the street were shocked, but not as shocked as this man was. I grabbed him and shook him in defense of the child."

When the man backed down, Danita gathered up the children and fed them. "I walked away with tears streaming down my face. I knew I would never be the same."

An Unlikely Missionary

The Christian school became Danita's initiation into ministry. Grateful for the help, they gave her a place to sleep—a cot in a classroom. "Those months were hard," she said as she toured the grounds recently, with dozens of school children hugging her. "Back then, the school had no electricity. [It now has a generator.]

So when it got dark, it got real dark. The only bathroom was across a dirt 'hallway' and behind a locked door.

"In total darkness, alone in the middle of the night, little noises became big noises. I had no way to know if there was a pig outside or someone who might harm me. If I turned on a flashlight, the bugs would attack the light, so thick in the air, I was almost breathing them."

But Danita had a vision. "I wanted to open an orphanage, to take in only children who had lost their parents, children like the ones begging for scraps at that restaurant."

For many months she lived in that schoolroom, with only her prayer life to chase away her fears in the dark and keep alive her dream to rescue children. Then finally last fall, a building came available. Built by a somewhat wealthy family (by Haitian standards) as a future retirement home, the modest stucco building had more to offer than even Danita knew at the time.

Less than half a mile from the Dominican Republic border, the home offered needed access to relative civilization on the "other side." In the Dominican Republic there are grocery stores, phones, lights and places to eat.

Danita signed a lease for $450 and moved in alone. On Christmas Eve 1999, she spent the night all by herself in that empty dark house. She went from cot to cot, praying for the children she knew God would soon send her way.

"One verse became my mission verse: 'Open your mouth for the speechless, in the cause of all who are appointed to die. Open your mouth, judge righteously, and plead the cause of the poor and needy'" (PROV. 31:8-9, NKJV).

By Christmas 2000, the verse came alive as every bed was filled. Happy laughter of children celebrating Christmas for the first time filled the air. There were toys and carols, good food and smiles.

And there was one other sign that the outreach was growing. In the street was an eight-foot panel truck, painted bright yellow with the Metro Ministries logo on the side. Bill Wilson of the well-known Brooklyn, New York, ministry raised the money to buy this truck so Danita could also do sidewalk Sunday school.

"Bill has been my greatest encourager. From day one, he said to me, 'I know you can do this.' He gave me advice that no money can buy. He got us this truck that has allowed me to minister to hundreds of children outside our doors.

"All I have to do is park this truck, open it up and start the sound system. I have a crowd so large, so fast that I have to ask the parents to step back and bring the children forward so they can hear."

Wilson speaks of Danita in a quiet hush: "She reminds me of me when I was 30 years old and people told me I couldn't start a ministry in New York. That was in the days where there was no inner-city work. But I did it, and Danita is going to do it too."

As Danita walks through the mud hut village behind the children's home, an older woman walks up to her, holding the hand of a naked child, no more than 3 years old. They converse, and Danita shakes her head. "The woman wants to give the baby to me," she explains. "It happens all the time. Parents here try to pass off their children so there is one less mouth to feed, more food to go around. It is all about survival.

"But my heart is for orphans. Pastors from the churches around here bring me children when their parents die," she says, pausing. "And they die young here. A few months ago, a pastor came to me because a young mother had died in her sleep. She was only 32 years old. She wasn't sick; she just died.

"The father was unable to care for the children alone, so he brought me his four children. The oldest was 8, and the youngest was only 6 months old. As I was getting the children settled, I asked the father for some basic information. When he started telling me the children's names, he stopped. He had to ask the oldest what the baby's name was."

Children left at the orphanage show no signs of separation anxiety—just the opposite. For the first time in their young lives, they have meals, regular wholesome meals. They have clothes to wear and shoes for their feet. Well fed and cared for, the children are then ready to learn. Every day, the children are taught basic education and that God loves them.

This part of her ministry extends beyond the 26 children who call the orphanage home. Danita visited the homes nearest her and found 50 other children who were not attending school.

"Here in Haiti, there is public school, but it is very overcrowded and badly run. Worse, you have to buy books and a uniform to attend. So if a child's parents can't afford these—and most can't—they stay home."

Danita handpicked her 50 students from those unable to attend public school. They lived closest to her—most literally a stone's throw away.

She started her own school, where the children are also taught about Jesus. "It's not enough to just learn about the Lord in Sunday school when you live in these conditions. They need daily instruction if it is going to make a difference."

Suffering Children

Life is hard for the people of Haiti, but even more so for the children—especially the sick ones.

"One of my little boys has always been sickly. His name is Gee, and he is 4 years old. His mother had died. Gee had no one but his little sister.

"Almost from the first day he was here, I started taking him to the doctor. But medical care here is really terrible, and he kept getting even sicker. Finally, I was so frightened for him that I got a permit to take him to Santo Domingo, a torturous five-hour bus drive.

"Since he didn't have a passport, the legal red tape and delays dragged on. Finally they admitted him and found he had [tuberculosis] and was HIV-positive."

The doctor was very direct with Danita: "Just leave him here to die. It's not your baby. Why put yourself through this?"

Horrified at the thought of leaving this poor, sick child alone to die, Danita settled in for a few days at what was known as the Dominican's finest children's hospital.

"They took us to a ward, a huge room filled with 14 children. Most of them had been abandoned by their parents," she says. "I guess when you have four children, and one is sick, and the other three will starve if you stay with the dying one, you feel you have no choice. My heart broke for these children.

"Worse—the nurses there are so overworked and understaffed that they must depend on the parents to care for their children. But if the child is abandoned, then they look to the other mothers to care for the sickest children as well as their own."

But most of the children had no one. "I remember the doctor walking in one night and standing over a frail little girl. 'Has anyone fed this child today?' she asked. The other mothers and I looked at one another. One had given her juice, but that was all. The child had not been fed for only God knows how long.

"The nurses came in and asked if one of us would help hold a 5-year-old girl named Erica so that she could put an IV in her. This little girl was HIV-positive, and there was no one to care for her.

"I held her close as the nurse tried over and over to find a vein. The baby would scream with all her might and fight to get away from the pain. I lost count after the nurse stuck that baby for the ninth time. Her cries filled the room as the woman callously poked and prodded with the sharp needle. Finally I couldn't do it any more. The nurse gave up with a shrug and turned without a backward glance, 'Let her die in peace.'"

The next day, the girl died alone in her filthy bed. Danita left the hospital with Gee hours later. The hospital offered no help, no hope.

"As I packed Gee's bag and fled that terrible place, I started praying a prayer I refused to give up: 'Lord Jesus, these children need a clinic, with a doctor that cares, with medicine and clean instruments. Father, speak to a nurse or doctor to come here and care for these babies.'"

Though it would be easy to be discouraged, Danita has a vision of what God will do. She looks over her orphanage and speaks with conviction. "See this field," she says as she waves her hand over an empty lot, littered with trash."Last year, the Lord spoke to me to buy this land. I took out a loan for $10,000 with no idea how I could pay it. But I knew this land was vital to our future. It is right behind the orphanage, the only available land for us to grow and for the children to have a place to play.

"A few weeks later I was in New York, and a woman who I had never met gave me an anonymous gift that was enough to pay off the loan, plus buy shoes and uniforms for all of my children. There will be a medical clinic here one day so my children will have real care. There will be a playground so that my children can run and jump and climb in safety. Every child needs a place to play, and right now, all we have is the street...but we will have a playground someday."

Just a short time ago, the lights went on for the first time at the Hope for Haiti orphanage as a donated generator was finally installed. That also brought running water to the home.

Another blessing was Nancy Soto, another woman who had "every excuse" not to be a missionary. She has committed one year to living at Hope for Haiti and pouring herself into Danita's children. At press time Nancy was taking legal steps to adopt the youngest orphan, Rose Marie.

The most urgent need facing the home now is acquiring the building they are in. "I signed a lease that allowed me to rent it for a few more months, but if I don't buy it for $75,000 by the end of the lease, they will sell it to someone else. Several people have approached the owner expressing an interest, so we have to raise these funds quickly."

For someone who had every excuse not to be a missionary, Danita has done a remarkable job. And it's just the beginning—a wonderful example of what one life can do.

Bio
Mary Hutchinson is a writer based in Boston. Christian Life Missions is raising funds to help Danita's orphanage. Tax-deductible gifts can be made payable to Christian Life Missions, P.O. Box 952248, Lake Mary, FL 32795-2248, marked "Hope for Haiti."